MUNCH

MUNCH

Hein Scholtz

PHOTOGRAPHY: WARREN HEATH | FOOD STYLING: BRITA DU PLESSIS

Published in 2013 by Struik Lifestyle
(an imprint of Random House Struik (Pty) Ltd)
Company Reg. No 1966/003153/07
Wembley Square, First Floor, Solan Road,
Gardens, Cape Town 8001
PO Box 1144 Cape Town 8000 South Africa

www.randomstruik.co.za

ISBN 978 143170 291 6

Publisher: Linda de Villiers
Managing editor: Cecilia Barfield
Design manager: Beverley Dodd
Editor: Bronwen Leak
Designer: Helen Henn
Photographer: Warren Heath
Photographer's assistant: Michael Leveson
Food stylist: Brita du Plessis
Food stylist's assistant: Yvette Pascoe
Proofreader: Gill Gordon
Indexer: Bronwen Leak

Reproduction: Hirt & Carter Cape (Pty) Ltd
Printing and binding: 1010 Printing International
Ltd, China

ACKNOWLEDGEMENTS

This book is surely dedicated to all of you out there who have, at times, been clueless as to what to make for breakfast, lunch, dinner – even a snack. To the reader – this book is for you, to help you on your own culinary adventure.

This book is also dedicated to my dad, who passed away due to cancer in 2009. He taught me how to slaughter a sheep when I was eight and to be a braaimaster before puberty hit. No bets as to where I got my love of food from.

A shout-out to the production team – Linda, thanks for believing in a young dude with flip-flops and a goofy grin, Helen for your patience and project management prowess, Bronwen for your help when words failed me, and to Warren, Brita, Yvette, Mike, Julia and, of course, the host with the most, Marc, for lending us your lovely Obz home to shoot in!

I am eternally grateful for my bevy of friends, for their support, 'likes', 'shares' and tweets, and for my family members who showed love with their kind words and inquisitive calls.

Werner, thanks for the videos, the shared late nights, and for being there!

Here's to a good life guys,
@heinscholtz

CONTENTS

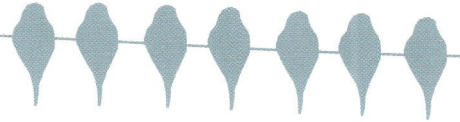

INTRODUCTION

It's amazing how, for someone who has so much to say about food, I struggled to find the words to start the introduction to my very own cookbook.

Like with most things, I guess it would be best to start with the basics: I love food.

Food brings people together. It nourishes. It's colourful and inspires creativity and alchemy. But let's get real for a second. It all boils down to taste. If something tastes good, your mouth salivates. You close your eyes when you take the first few bites. You go back for seconds. You get excited to eat it. You tell people about it. These are the moments in life that I cherish, when the food I eat not only fills my stomach, but makes me experience a whole host of different sensations.

But for a lot of people, food also brings frustration ... something I first experienced when I moved out of my parents' house at the tender age of 19, to study at university. In the dining hall of the university residence, I gained a healthy respect for the food my mother prepared – even the stuff I hadn't liked, longing for it when compared to some of the fare I was served in my first year.

I wasn't alone. We did a poll once in res and I remember someone talking about how unsurprising it was that the majority of students didn't like res food, even though they were paying a great deal of money for the service. What's more, only a small percentage of students are lucky enough to have res placement – the vast majority live in private accommodation. These kids face an even bigger hurdle: to fend for themselves when it comes to mealtimes.

Food is forever on a student's mind. What will I have for lunch? What takeaway looks good? Can I afford that? What groceries should I buy this week? Can I make this in my small oven/microwave? Organic, grain fed, free range – should I care? How do I carry my sandwich to class without squishing it? Do I always have to eat the same things?

We were forever complaining about what we were eating. My friends looked forward to going home because then they could get home-cooked meals. Being from Namibia, I had no such luck. I had to feed myself on long weekends and holidays. When we moved out of res, the situation didn't improve for most of us. During the week my friends would either live on takeaways or buy something every day on the way home from class. I remember thinking to myself how expensive an exercise it was – I sure as hell didn't have enough money to do that. So I asked some of them why they always bought their meals – even when eating at home – and the answer startled me: they didn't really know what else to do.

I was shocked, but it got me thinking.

You see, even though I too was now living in private accommodation, I had loved learning and experimenting in the kitchen when I was a child at home. This had allowed me to just carry on when I started out on my own. I realised how lucky I was. For a sizeable chunk of the student population, food preparation extends to making a sandwich or quickly boiling two-minute noodles.

Living on my own gave me a chance to start forming my own food habits – habits I will in all likelihood retain for the rest of my life. So, being what most people term a *foodie* (I liken it to being a sports fanatic, only I play my matches in the kitchen and on the braai and not necessarily on the sports field), I dedicated my student years to trying out dishes that were not only tasty, nutritious and healthy, but also student-friendly.

I held dinner parties, cooked romantic meals, made my own 'fast food', bought groceries (that I actually used), made stews, sandwiches and sweet things, and braaied. I did all these things on a modest student budget, and all in a reasonable time. Although I ate out a lot (my other hobby, besides experimenting with my own food, is to enjoy the triumphs of others), I usually ate at home or made sure there was something to eat when I had to be home. This also meant I almost always made lunch for myself, making the pull of the food shops in student centres less magnetic. My wallet still thanks me, as do my taste buds.

These self-taught food habits and recipes also saved my tuchus when I started working, since the student lifestyle closely mirrors that of a young professional (the most notable difference being that there is even less time to cook, and not much of a budget to work with initially).

And this is ultimately the idea behind this cookbook.

I want to help you form your own healthy food habits; to not just rely on ready-made and expensive meals – either gourmet from your local upmarket grocery store or takeaways from your favourite pizza joint – but to develop your palate and make your own food. I want to help you solve the mid-week lunch crises, to host cheaply, and even just to get started. I am not saying that you won't eat two-minute noodles now and then, or that you won't stretch the limits of the various uses of canned tuna or baked beans. Instead, the recipes in this book are also for when you decide to do something different, something a little out of the ordinary. That's not to say you can't cook them every night. I have been using these since my first year away from home.

My wish for you – whether you are a student, a young person who has just left home and started working, or even someone who just bought this cookbook because you found it interesting – is that you allow yourself to enjoy it. Enjoy making food. Enjoy eating it. Life really is about the small things.

Now go and introduce yourself to your kitchen, no matter how small it is. ;-)

 @heinscholtz

INITIATION

With regards to the format of this book, you will notice a social media theme. The reason behind this is quite simple really, and it has to do with the fact that all I really want is to help you discover your inner foodie.

Each recipe has a hash tag (#) that will allow you to comment on that particular recipe on Twitter. Here you can share your own (and your guests') experiences with the dish, post photos of variations, suggest and advise, or just make friends with other people who have tweeted the same recipe. You are welcome to follow me on Twitter too – if you want to ask me anything or talk about anything food related, feel free! Follow me on @heinscholtz and @MunchSA.

You'll also find QR codes on some pages, which will link you to a few interesting websites related to the recipe, additional pictures of the dish or even a quick video when it comes to a technique that might be hard to explain to the novice cook. You'll be able to read and see more both on Facebook and @MunchSA.

It's all about interaction – I hope to get you talking about and making food!

THE STARTER KITCHEN

Moving into a digs, your own place or even a residence is probably one of the most significant steps you'll ever take. It's the human version of getting kicked out of the nest and learning to fly. Some of us do it early on in life and others only later. What we all have in common, however, is the rare chance to start over and go it alone. What is also rare is the opportunity to start afresh in your kitchen, with no utensil or grocery baggage. And if you choose and shop smartly, you'll always have what you need.

KITCHEN POWER TOOLS

I remember when I was a first year. Coming from Namibia, where I guess we are famous for eating nothing but meat, my dad said he would get me a set of 15 cutting knives. I had a knife for everything. And what's more, the set was on special! Sounded like a good deal at the time, yes? Problem was that I never even used half of them. And their quality was so poor that I had to replace the ones I did use in that first year. The lesson learnt? It is better to spend a little more on a little less, especially when it comes to kitchen utensils.

Being a student doesn't mean you must only work with shoddy-quality utensils. It doesn't mean your money is worth any less than a working person's. When I realised this, I threw away the remainder of the knives I owned (by my second year they were coming out of their black plastic handles or were discolouring) and spent the same amount of money on only three knives, and they still work well for me to this day.

Being a student or young professional does not have the same connotation it had a few decades ago, where you had the bare minimum of appliances and having your own toaster was a luxury. This is not the assumption that this cookbook makes. I will assume you have at least two hotplates and either a combination microwave/oven or a separate microwave and oven. A toaster is a given, and so is a kettle. But there is a plethora of other kitchen things, and you never really know if you will use them unless you buy them.

What follows is my suggestion for your starter kitchen, to help you sort out the clutter from the really necessary items:

- 1 large casserole or roasting pan – preferably non-stick (for big, decadent roasts)
- 1 medium-sized or large saucepan (it's not necessary to get a small one unless you are into making sauces, or pedantic about making flapjacks or saucer-shaped eggs)
- 1 small cooking pot with lid
- 1 large cooking pot with lid (large enough to hold at least 2 litres water)
- 1 non-stick metal baking tray (large enough for a pizza to fit on)
- 1 non-stick muffin pan (for larger muffins, unless you want to make cupcakes)
- 1 non-stick cake pan (with a loose bottom for easy lifting)
- 1 large colander/sieve
- egg lifter/spatula
- whisk
- soup ladle
- pasta scoop
- pestle and mortar
- wooden spoons (1 small, 1 large)
- serrated butcher's knife

- smooth-blade butcher's knife
- filleting knife
- multisided grater
- peeler
- 6 knives (if you get serrated knives then you don't need steak knives – they also look classier)
- 6 forks
- 6 spoons (you won't really need soup spoons specifically unless you prefer their shape to normal tablespoons)
- 8–12 teaspoons
- 2 large metal serving spoons
- 6–8 plates
- 4 cups and 4 mugs (sometimes you want a swimming pool to drink out of)
- 4 medium-sized wine glasses (no need to get large ones for red and smaller ones for white unless you are a budding sommelier)
- 6–8 general drinking glasses (try 4 tumblers and 4 tall glasses)

When it comes to plastic containers, make sure they are the right size for you to carry with you to class or work. I suggest you get at least five, including a few larger ones for storing leftovers in the fridge. Some food will require a brown paper bag, clingfilm or aluminium foil, so make sure you find out what works for you. I usually wrap sandwiches and wraps in clingfilm and put them in a brown paper bag that can go into my work bag. Leftover stews, roasts or salads work better when put in plastic containers – just always put them into a plastic Ziploc bag too because you never know when the lid might come loose and spill the contents all over your MacBook or class notes!

HUNTING & GATHERING

There are food items I have realised that are always a good idea to keep in your kitchen. These are things that can either save you when your attempt at budgeting starts failing as you near the end of the month, or that you can literally base a dish on. The point is that if you make sure you always have these things in your kitchen, you will be only a grocery or two away from most meals.

IN THE FRIDGE

- eggs
- milk (I prefer full-cream)
- unsalted butter (non-negotiable – you can't cook with margarine, no matter what they say)
- potatoes
- onions (never keep onions and potatoes together – the onions release sulphur dioxide which makes the potatoes go off quicker; by the same token, never keep bananas in the fridge – the skin will go black and the flesh will go pulpy)
- tomatoes
- lemons
- fresh garlic
- fresh ginger
- water (it's always good to keep a water container in the fridge – glass is the best option but plastic works too, just replace the bottle more often – I often use leftover wine bottles to store water)
- jam (always in a glass jar with a lid – don't store it in the can it may have come in)
- frozen corn and peas
- puff pastry
- vodka (is there any other way to store it?)

Most condiments, like tomato sauce and mayonnaise, need to be refrigerated once opened. And always remember to close the lids properly. There's nothing worse than sour, runny tomato sauce when you need it most!

IN THE PANTRY

- white cake flour (try to always keep 500 g at any given time)
- baking powder (refill with the sachets – it's much cheaper)
- bicarbonate of soda
- brown sugar (I almost never use white sugar except when baking)
- vanilla extract (you don't really need the pods – just try and get the extract, and not essence)
- peanut butter (not only nutritious and tasty as a snack, but comes in handy when baking and making Asian-inspired dishes too)
- Marmite/Oxo/Bovril (whichever one you prefer – they come in handy when making stocks or used instead of salt, and are great for their vitamin content, and also as a spread on toast when you have a sore tummy)

- soy sauce (if you have high blood pressure I suggest going low sodium, lest you get a heart attack at 26)
- extra-virgin olive oil (it has become more inexpensive these days, and it's so healthy for you)
- sunflower oil (now and then you need to use this type of oil because it handles higher temperatures better than olive oil, like in stir-fries)
- fine iodised table salt
- coarse sea salt (in a grinder, or Maldon salt if you really want to go all out)
- black peppercorns (in a grinder – never the fine powder, it loses its kick in that state)
- canned tomatoes (even better than using fresh tomatoes for sauces and stews – when in doubt, rather go canned when making stews)
- rice (I use brown and wild rice)
- pasta (I prefer linguine or vermicelli)
- oats
- baked beans in tomato sauce (I prefer Heinz or Koo)
- muesli (great for breakfast, great for baking; see my recipe on page 25)

When it comes to fruit, try to buy what is in season. Even though apples can be found throughout the year, you'll find they taste better (and their nutritional content is higher) when in season. Bananas, oranges (and their more easily peel-able hybrids) and apples are staples you should always aim to have in your kitchen. Apples are better than a cup of coffee to wake you up in the morning, and bananas give you sustained energy throughout the day (and are a great source of fibre), while both help curb your appetite. Oranges are full of vitamin C which is great for your immune system.

If you are unfortunate enough to dislike eating fruit, you could always invest in a blender and add two fruits to some ice, yoghurt and muesli for your fruit fix, be it as a morning shake or a post-gym energy fix (see recipe on page 25).

FOR YOUR INFORMATION

The purpose of this page is to inform you about the food trends and related topics that you will invariably come across. Don't get duped by clever marketing; know what it is that you are buying. It's important to understand how and why what you put in your mouth affects your body. Here are some of the most talked-about concepts. The rest you can find by following me on Twitter – you are welcome to tweet me any questions!

all grain: Refers to poultry, mostly chicken, and that their diet includes multiple grain varieties. Eggs can also be termed all grain, and it is associated with a more nutritious product.

free range: A response to battery chickens and the way certain animals, reared for human consumption, are treated. It works on the supposition that if an animal eats a more natural diet, and is happier in behaving in a natural way (instead of not being able to move its entire life while getting fat in a small cage), then its products (e.g. meat or eggs) will taste better. That and soothe our conscience.

glycaemic index (GI): High-GI foods are broken down faster in our bodies and, as such, give us an energy spike, but also leave us hungry sooner than low-GI foods that are broken down more slowly, giving us sustained energy. If coupled with high-fibre foods, we feel fuller for longer. I find it best to eat a mixed-GI breakfast, a low-GI lunch and a medium-to-high GI dinner. If you snack in between, it's best to go for medium-GI snacks. In this way, you maintain a constant energy flow without spiking and causing tiredness. If you incorporate fibre as a snack, like a banana, this will work even better.

metabolism: The rate at which your body burns fuel. All the food you eat is so that your body can burn the fats, proteins and carbohydrates to give you energy to do stuff.

organic: This term is widely misunderstood and has been hijacked by clever marketers to sell anything these days. Organic basically means that the product has been reared or grown in conditions that mimic its natural growth, which means no human intervention regarding hormones, pesticides or fertilisers. It does not necessarily mean you will get a better product, but rather that the environment was minimally impacted to get the product to you. It is more expensive, but is worth it when you are buying dairy products and meat.

seasonality: In this day and age, there are so many ways of preserving food that we can get most fruits and vegetables, and even meat, all year round. Originally, things were only available 'in season', when fruits and vegetables ripened naturally during certain seasons, or certain animals were at their peak to be slaughtered. Now fruits and vegetables are either imported from where they are in season (e.g. avocados from Spain) or are harvested unripened and stored until the produce goes out of season. This produce is then artificially ripened by tinkering with temperatures and exposing it to certain gases. The problems with this are that imported food is more expensive (so you should always try to buy from local sources) and food that has been artificially ripened hasn't got anywhere near the same amount of nutritional value as naturally ripened food. Not to mention that it tastes noticeably less fresh and more mundane.

For more on food trends or any questions, tweet me. If you want to know something specific – I'll try to help where I can!

7 WAYS WITH EGGS

& SOME OTHER BREKKIE IDEAS

Eggs have gotten a bad rap in the past, and it's quite unfair really. You'd need to eat at least two eggs every day to negatively influence your cholesterol — and that is if you are already prone to high cholesterol levels. Eggs actually make a healthy meal, being very high in protein specifically. They are cheap, plentiful, always in season and versatile, so it makes sense for them to feature quite prominently in a student cookbook. I always use free-range eggs. You can use grain-fed too; I just find that free-range eggs taste better, as well as have a healthier-looking yolk.

Here are seven ways to cook eggs, and a few suggestions on how to eat them. All the recipes are cheap, relatively easy and quick to prepare, and serve one person (unless otherwise stated).

BOILED EGGS

What could be more classic than a boiled egg with toast soldiers? This is my variation.

INGREDIENTS
2 eggs
pinch of salt
2 thick slices toast, lightly buttered on both sides
salt and freshly ground black pepper to taste
1 Tbsp strawberry jam
sprig of fresh thyme, chopped

WHAT TO DO

1. Put the eggs in a saucepan, add the pinch of salt and just cover them with lukewarm water. Put the pan on a hotplate and bring to the boil.
2. Boil for 3 minutes, then remove from the heat, pour out the hot water and cover in cold water and pour out again. Leave for 5 minutes to cool then remove the eggs from the water and leave to dry.
3. Hold an egg in the palm of your hand and lightly tap it on a hard surface on all sides, then softly roll it on the surface, applying some pressure just to break the shell. Peel off the shell with the thin membrane.
4. Cut off the crusts of the warm toast and then cut the toast in 4 slices each, lengthways – making 'fingers'.
5. Make a little construction on your plate of the 8 toast fingers, leaving a rectangular opening in the middle for the eggs.
6. Slice the eggs and place in the small cavity (the egg yolks should be oozing out slowly). Season to taste.
7. Microwave the strawberry jam in a small bowl and pour around the egg and toast. Sprinkle over the thyme.

> **TIP** The toast 'finger' construction helps to soak up the warm egg yolk, and provides a way for you to eat with your fingers if you want. This is a very playful way of eating this dish. Alternatively, you can just eat the egg with a teaspoon and some strawberry jam on toast.

SCRAMBLED EGGS

This recipe is a sure-fire way to make scrambled egg the way it should be done – and to enjoy it!

INGREDIENTS
2 eggs
pinch of salt
1 Tbsp water or milk
1 slice toast
1 small ripe avocado, sliced or mashed
1 tomato, sliced
2 basil leaves, shredded
small dollop of butter
freshly ground black pepper to taste

WHAT TO DO

1. Break the eggs into a small mixing bowl and whisk enough to break the yolks and mix with the egg whites – not too much. Add a pinch of salt and the water or milk. Whisk until mixed.
2. Top the toast with the avocado, tomato and basil.
3. Melt the butter in a small pan on high heat and add the eggs.
4. Whisk every 10 seconds as the eggs gradually cook to keep the bottom from burning. When about half the scrambled egg is cooked and the other half is still runny, turn off the heat and whisk until the scrambled egg is finely scrambled, and still rather wet, but firm. From eggs into the pan until ready should take just less than 2 minutes.
5. Serve the avocado and tomato toast with the scrambled eggs on the side, with pepper to taste.

> **TIP** Scrambled egg can be so tempting that at times you just want to eat it by itself – and that's fine! Otherwise, serve it with bacon and toast with marmalade, or with smoked trout on a croissant. You can even have it on toast with some cream or smooth cottage cheese – as long as you enjoy it!

FRIED EGGS

Sometimes there is nothing as pleasing as frying an egg for a light meal. Here's a quick recipe that not only makes a great fried egg, but also brings out the flavour of the other ingredients. A pinch of rosemary salt really makes this special.

INGREDIENTS

½ tsp coarse or Maldon salt
sprig of fresh rosemary, chopped
1 large or 2 medium Portabellini mushrooms (you can use any mushroom that is in season, like King Oyster or Porcini)
1 slice ciabatta, sliced widthways (also works well with a large slice of rye loaf)
½ tsp butter or small glug of olive oil
2 eggs
2 large slices smoked ham (Black Forest works well)
2 slices Emmental cheese
freshly ground black pepper to taste

WHAT TO DO

1. In a pestle and mortar, grind the salt and rosemary together. Set aside.
2. Slice the mushrooms lengthways, 4–6 slices depending on the size of the mushroom. Brush some olive oil on the slice of bread.
3. Heat a frying pan and add the butter or olive oil. Fry the mushrooms until cooked through (about 3 minutes). Set aside.
4. Use the same pan to toast your ciabatta slice. Set aside.
5. Now crack the egg shells gently on a hard surface and gently pour the eggs into the pan so that the yolks don't break. Fry the eggs on medium heat for 40–60 seconds, then cover the pan with a lid to make sure the egg whites cook, without burning the edges of the eggs. After another minute, remove from the stove. The egg yolks should be semi-set, and the whites cooked through.
6. Transfer the ciabatta to a plate and cover it first with the slices of smoked ham, then the mushrooms, and finally the cheese. Place the freshly made fried eggs on top.
7. Sprinkle with rosemary salt and freshly ground black pepper to taste.

> **TIP** Some people like fried eggs with a pork chop — a mixed grill, they call it! Other ways of trying out your egg-frying technique is on toast with a few thick slices of mature Cheddar cheese, and some Tabasco sauce blotted on top. Even Marmite toast with a fried egg on top fills the gap sometimes — whichever way you do it, enjoy it!

7 WAYS WITH EGGS

POACHED EGGS

This is not a conventional way to cook eggs, but it is a great way to mix it up a little. You sort of pat yourself on the shoulder because it looks so difficult and fancy, but is actually so easy to make. The perfect breakfast to impress on a lazy Sunday morning!

INGREDIENTS
1 large overripe tomato, cubed
2 small spring onions, thinly sliced
sprig of fresh thyme, finely chopped
½ tsp olive oil
juice of ½ lemon
salt and freshly ground black pepper to taste
non-stick cooking spray
2 eggs
½ small French loaf, sliced lengthways
dollop of mustard
3–4 slices salami
baby spinach leaves, or anything green in your fridge (optional)

WHAT TO DO
1. Place the tomato, onions and thyme in a small mixing bowl. Add the olive oil and lemon juice, and season to taste. Set aside.
2. Now cut an A4-sized piece of clingfilm and place it over a soup bowl. Spray the clingfilm with cooking spray. Break 1 egg carefully over the clingfilm, add a small pinch of salt and gather the clingfilm into a knot at the top. Repeat with the other egg.
3. Toast the bread slices in a hot frying pan on both sides.
4. Bring a saucepan of water to the boil, turn down the heat to medium and submerge the clingfilm eggs, using a spoon to keep them underwater. Let them cook for 2–3 minutes before removing them from the water and placing them carefully in the soup bowl to rest.
5. Smear the bread slices with mustard and top with the salami, followed by the leaves if using. Arrange the slices on a plate and drop dollops of the tomato salsa evenly over them. Lastly, carefully add the poached eggs from the clingfilm with a large spoon. Season to taste.

> **TIP** A classic way of eating poached eggs is with some ham on an English muffin, drenched in Hollandaise sauce. Make this quick 'cheats' Hollandaise: Place 2 egg yolks, a glug of olive oil, a dollop of mustard, a pinch of salt and some water to thin it out a little bit in a saucepan, and cook over medium heat for at least 5 minutes while whisking continuously for a smooth consistency.

7 WAYS WITH EGGS

OMELETTE

There is something to be said for a quick omelette: tucking into a fabulously rich meal with a delicious filling. The great thing about an omelette is that it isn't just perfect for brunch, but for any time of the day when you are home and feel snackish. Feel free to play around with fillings – this recipe is just a guideline.

INGREDIENTS
½ **chorizo sausage, sliced**
2 **slices strong Cheddar cheese**
3 **chives, finely chopped**
2 **eggs**
1 **Tbsp full-cream milk, cream or smooth cottage cheese**
salt and freshly ground black pepper to taste
dollop of butter

WHAT TO DO
1. Prepare the chorizo, cheese and chives.
2. Break the eggs into a mixing bowl, add the milk (or cream or cottage cheese) and a pinch of salt, and mix until combined (don't overmix).
3. Melt the butter in a medium non-stick frying pan with a lid. As soon as the butter starts darkening, add the egg mixture and turn the heat down to medium. As soon as the bottom of the egg mixture has set and only the top part is runny, use a spatula to loosen the edges. Put on the lid for 10 seconds at a time to make sure the top starts cooking and congealing. Turn off the heat at this stage.
4. When the omelette's surface is still slightly runny but basically almost cooked, add the chorizo, cheese and half the chopped chives in a line from top to bottom in the middle of the omelette. Season with salt and pepper. Do this all very quickly before the omelette cooks too dry.
5. Loosen the sides of the omelette with a spatula, fold one half over the other, and slide it onto a plate. Sprinkle over the rest of the chives and enjoy!

> TIP You can add salami or any type of sausage to this dish if you are not a fan of the paprika-flavoured chorizo. Other quick fillings for an omelette include:
> * smoked trout ribbons, rocket leaves, sliced olives or capers, and smooth cottage cheese;
> * grated mature Cheddar cheese, fried mushrooms and chopped tomatoes; or
> * bacon, grated Cheddar cheese and honey.

FRENCH TOAST

French toast is so popular at the moment, but everyone seems to be sticking to the typical French toast with syrup and cheese that some of us grew up with. Here is a great recipe that works well on weekends when you have mates over from the previous evening's shenanigans. A whole, medium-sized French loaf should serve about four people, but this recipe only serves one.

INGREDIENTS

2 eggs
1 Tbsp finely grated hard salty cheese (e.g. Pecorino, Gruyère, Parmesan, or any cheese if you are making this on a whim)
salt and freshly ground black pepper to taste
3 rashers bacon
3 thick slices French loaf, cut breadthways
3 thin slices white Gouda, mild white Cheddar or Emmental cheese
1 overripe tomato, sliced
3 large basil leaves
dollop of honey

WHAT TO DO

1. Break the eggs into a mixing bowl, add the grated cheese, season to taste (not too much salt if using a salty hard cheese) and whisk.
2. Heat a frying pan and fry the bacon until crispy. Remove the bacon from the pan but don't turn off the heat. (For even crispier bacon, grill it in the oven.)
3. Dip the slices of French loaf into the egg and soak them for 10 seconds or so before putting them into the hot pan. Turn the heat to medium and fry the slices until nicely browned on both sides and the egg is cooked through (about 1 minute per side).
4. Top each French toast with a slice of cheese and tomato, a basil leaf and a rasher of bacon. Lastly, drizzle with honey and season to taste.

> **TIP** Most people I know just pour syrup over their French toast and enjoy it just like that. It can be made with any sliced bread – just be careful not to let it lie in the batter too long, otherwise it will fall apart.

FRITTATA

A frittata is like a light quiche – some might call it a deconstructed omelette – but, however you want to describe it, it's another example of how versatile eggs can be! This is a rather large dish that could be shared by two people.

INGREDIENTS
½ **red sweet/bell pepper, deseeded and cubed**
olive oil
3 eggs, separated
⅓ **cup grated cheese or crumbled feta**
handful of baby spinach leaves, chopped
2–3 slices cooked or smoked ham, diced
freshly ground black pepper to taste

WHAT TO DO

1. Fry the red pepper cubes in some olive oil in a medium non-stick frying pan for about 3 minutes until tender. Set aside to cool in a small mixing bowl (you can place them in the fridge to cool).

2. Once cool, add the egg yolks, cheese, spinach and ham, and season with pepper to taste. Mix thoroughly.

3. Beat the egg whites in a large mixing bowl until soft peaks form.

4. Using a large metal spoon, carefully fold a third of the beaten egg whites into the egg-yolk filling. When mixed, gently fold in the other two thirds of the egg whites so that they are evenly distributed. Work lightly, to keep the air in the mixture.

5. Reheat the pan on high heat and gently add the mixture, evenly distributing the filling.

6. Cover with a lid and cook for about 2 minutes, checking every 15 seconds – as soon as the edges turn golden brown, and the top is almost cooked but still soft and slightly runny, loosen the sides with a spatula and flip to cook the other side. If you don't want to risk it, just leave the lid on to make sure the frittata is cooked all the way through – this will take another minute – but switch to medium heat to make sure the bottom of the frittata doesn't burn.

7. When cooked, loosen the sides and bottom of the frittata, and slide onto a plate.

> **TIP** You can use whatever you like as a filling, such as mince and peas, chicken pieces with sweetcorn, or feta with sundried tomatoes and bacon bits.

7 WAYS WITH EGGS

MUESLI

Store-bought muesli can be expensive, so making it at home is well worth the effort. This recipe should give you 15 servings, so why not double it? (It will keep for a month.)

INGREDIENTS
3 cups rolled oats
1 cup sunflower seeds
1 cup pumpkin seeds
1 cup cashew nuts
1 Tbsp sunflower oil
2 Tbsp honey
pinch of salt
2 cups All-Bran flakes

WHAT TO DO
1. Preheat the oven to 200 °C.
2. Combine all the ingredients, except the All-Bran, and mix thoroughly.
3. Evenly spread out the mixture on a baking tray and bake for at least 20 minutes or until golden. You can grill it right at the end if you like a more golden muesli – just don't burn it!
4. Allow to cool before adding the All-Bran. Store in an airtight container.

> **TIP** You can have this muesli not only as a breakfast with yoghurt, but also as a snack or as a dessert with ice cream. I also crush it a little and add it to my rusk and cookie recipes.

BREAKFAST SHAKE

Okay, so not all of us have ample time in the morning to fix ourselves a proper breakfast. If you have a blender, sometimes it's nice just to throw a few things together and press 'blitz'. If this sounds like you, and you prefer drinking your breakfast, then give this a try.

INGREDIENTS
1 banana, peeled and sliced
1 apple, cored and diced
½ cup 100% fruit juice with bits (orange, strawberry, cranberry, whatever you prefer)
½ cup homemade muesli (see above)
½ cup natural, unsweetened Bulgarian yoghurt
½ cup ice

WHAT TO DO
1. Add everything to your blender and pulse first to get rid of the larger pieces, then blend to a smooth consistency.

> **TIP** The great thing about a blender is that you can blitz anything in it, and it gives you the perfect excuse to buy seasonal produce in bulk.

7 WAYS WITH EGGS

LIGHT MEALS
& SOME ACCOMPLISHED ACCOMPANIMENTS

Although I may not be the most vegan-dish-friendly person in the world, I do appreciate a salad now and then. This chapter includes, among other things, salads, some suggestions for sandwiches, as well as a few staple recipes like onion marmalade and guacamole. The salads are great as meals all by themselves, but also work as sides to a braai or any other main. The most important thing is that they are great to make the day before, or even the morning of, to take with you to class or work — as are the majority of the dishes in this cookbook.

QUICK ONION TART

This is an über-quick snack you can pop in the oven when unexpected guests stop by.

25–30 MINUTES | SERVES 4–6

INGREDIENTS
1 x 400 g roll frozen puff pastry, at room temperature
1 cup onion marmalade (see page 50)
100 g goat's milk or feta cheese
handful of rocket
4–6 thin slices Parma ham or any other smoked meat, snipped into slivers
1 avocado, thinly sliced

WHAT TO DO
1. Preheat the oven to 200 °C.
2. Gently roll out the pastry to fit a baking tray (too much handling will prevent the pastry from rising properly). Slice 2 cm-thick lengths off each side to create a border (build a wall) around the edges.
3. Put the pastry on a baking tray and spread with the onion marmalade.
4. Bake for 15–20 minutes or until the pastry is golden.
5. Crumble the cheese over the warm marmalade and top with the rocket and ham. Cut into small rectangles and serve with an avocado slice on each.

> TIP Try this with a tomato and mango basil salsa or a sweet pepper relish instead of onion marmalade — a sweet-and-savoury combination works well on puff pastry.

LIGHT MEALS

BUTTERNUT SOUP

This is a perennial favourite no matter the time of year. Although it needs the assistance of a handheld electric blender (which you can borrow from your neighbour if you haven't got one – in exchange for a cup of soup!) it is definitely worth the effort. You can use a typical potato masher – I have – and it will taste the same, but the vegetable bits may not be as fine as you would like. And don't worry that it makes such a lot – it freezes beautifully.

1 HOUR | SERVES **6–10**

INGREDIENTS
3 heaped tsp chicken stock powder or 2 cubes
4 cups boiling water
2 potatoes, peeled and diced
2 onions, peeled and diced
3 carrots, peeled and chopped
1 medium butternut, peeled and diced
1 tsp medium-strength curry powder
½ tsp paprika (if using smoked paprika, only add a pinch)
1 x 400 ml can coconut milk (shake the can to mix it thoroughly)
pinch of ground nutmeg
salt and freshly ground black pepper to taste

WHAT TO DO
1. Dissolve the stock in the boiling water in a large pot. Add the vegetables – they must be covered in water. If not, add enough extra water to cover them. Bring up to the boil, put on the lid and cook for about 30 minutes until the vegetables are soft. Stir every 5 minutes to prevent burning.
2. Reduce the heat and add the curry powder and paprika, and cook until all the vegetables are soft enough to blend or mash. Blend or mash the vegetables to the desired consistency.
3. Add the coconut milk (about three-quarters of the can to start, adding extra depending on how creamy you like it). Next add a pinch of nutmeg and some pepper. Only add salt if you need to.
4. Cook for a further 5–10 minutes over low heat. Serve as is with fresh rolls.

> TIP   This is also yummy with thin slices of smoked chicken added to it. Serving this with rolls with thin slices of mozzarella cheese melted over works wonders too!

LIGHT MEALS

MUSHROOM RISOTTO

Risotto is a dish associated with cold weather, comfort and indulgence. It's best nurtured with a glass of wine!

1 HOUR | SERVES 2—4

INGREDIENTS
3 shallots or 2 onions, peeled and diced
2 Tbsp butter
1 cup arborio rice
1 glass red wine
4 cups chicken stock
250 g seasonal mushrooms, sliced
olive oil
salt and freshly ground black pepper to taste
sprig of fresh thyme, finely chopped
50 ml cream

WHAT TO DO
1. Melt the butter in a large frying pan over medium heat and fry the shallots or onions for 5 minutes until translucent.
2. Add the rice and red wine and stir continuously. Add a ladleful of stock each time the risotto looks like it's getting too dry (rice soaks up moisture). Stir a few times every minute or so.
3. At the same time, fry the mushrooms in a little olive oil. Season with salt and pepper and add the thyme.
4. After 30 minutes, taste the rice. It should still have a bit of a bite to it, but should be almost cooked. Add the mushrooms and mix gently. Add cream a little at a time, just enough to make the risotto creamy but not running with cream.
5. Serve topped with a few shavings of a hard salty cheese like Parmesan.

> TIP   You can also try this risotto with white wine, cooked butternut and nutmeg.

LIGHT MEALS

NORTH AFRICAN COUSCOUS SALAD

Thanks to a deli I worked for when I was a student, I fell in love with this recipe. It will blow your socks off! Serve with a homemade hamburger instead of chips!

TAKES SOME TIME | SERVES **4**

INGREDIENTS
1 small butternut, peeled, deseeded and cubed into 2 cm cubes
1 tsp paprika
1 tsp sugar
pinch of salt
olive oil
2 cups couscous
3–4 Tbsp harissa paste
½ tsp aniseed
1 wheel feta cheese, crumbled
8 pickled peppadews, finely chopped, or 1 red sweet pepper,
  deseeded and finely cubed

WHAT TO DO
1. Heat the oven to 200 °C. Toss the butternut cubes in the paprika, sugar and salt, and then cover in olive oil. Spread out evenly on a baking tray and bake for about 40 minutes or until soft and approaching caramelisation.
2. Cook the couscous according to the packet instructions (usually 1½–2 cups salted boiling water to 1 cup couscous) and allow to cool.
3. Add a little olive oil to the harissa paste (I usually add ¼ cup olive oil), and add this to the couscous along with the aniseed. Mix carefully with a fork. Add the feta and butternut. Sprinkle over the peppadews and serve.

> TIP   I absolutely love the taste of this 'salad'. It works great as a main meal if you add some slices of smoked chicken, or even smoked snoek if you can get it.

LIGHT MEALS

SPINACH SALAD

I didn't like spinach as a kid – I'm still not a big fan, really. But when I discovered baby spinach, which you can get anywhere these days, I realised that the time had come to grow up. Just a little.

VERY QUICK | SERVES 1

INGREDIENTS
8–10 extra-thin slices smoked bacon, precooked
1 pkt baby spinach leaves, washed and patted dry
½ cup roasted sunflower or pumpkin seeds
1 cup cooked peas
1 Tbsp mayonnaise
1 Tbsp lemon juice
olive oil
salt and freshly ground black pepper to taste

> **TIP** Serve this either as a main meal or as a refreshing side salad to a pork fillet or gammon steaks.

WHAT TO DO
1. If you want, you can crisp the bacon in the oven under the grill.
2. Combine the bacon, spinach, seeds and peas in a salad bowl.
3. Whisk the mayonnaise and lemon juice with some olive oil and a little salt and pepper to make a dressing.

TUNA RICE SALAD

This is a great nutritious salad for summer.

QUICK | SERVES 1

INGREDIENTS
1 x 170 g can tuna, drained
1 ripe tomato, diced
2 cups cooked brown and wild rice
handful of rocket leaves, torn
glug of olive oil
1 Tbsp lemon juice
salt and freshly ground black pepper to taste

> **TIP** Leave out the rice and use as a topping for rice cakes or rye toast – add blue cheese or Camembert slices and, if you have any, cooked artichokes.

WHAT TO DO
1. Combine the tuna, tomato, rice and rocket in a salad bowl.
2. Drizzle with the olive oil and lemon juice, and season to taste.

LIGHT MEALS

BUTTER BEAN SALAD

A salad doesn't have to be just a few leaves and a smattering of sliced tomatoes. Sometimes it's nice to get out of your comfort zone and do something different, get different tastes going in your mouth. This salad, which is a meal in itself, is one of the cheapest to make. The addition of chorizo gives it a meaty touch.

10 MINUTES | SERVES **2**

INGREDIENTS
1 cup canned or cooked fresh peas
1 x 410 g can butter beans
½ chorizo sausage, thinly sliced
olive oil
salt and freshly ground black pepper to taste
1 tsp lemon juice
handful of fresh parsley, finely chopped, or 1 tsp dried
finely grated hard salty cheese, like Parmesan or Pecorino

WHAT TO DO
1. Drain the peas (if using canned) and butter beans, and wash gently in some cold water in a colander.
2. Heat a frying pan on high and sear the chorizo slices.
3. Toss the peas and butter beans in a salad bowl with some olive oil, salt and pepper, the lemon juice and parsley. Add the warm chorizo and a sprinkling of finely grated cheese, mix gently and serve.

> **TIP** You can substitute sugar beans, borlotti beans or chickpeas for the butter beans. You can also add a dollop of yoghurt, a few thinly sliced spring onions and some chopped fresh mint to make it into a nice salad for a braai.

BACON & CHICKPEA SALAD

Bacon in salad is, to me, almost a non-negotiable: the meaty, crispy, salty flavour is a most delicious surprise in a sea of fresh and juicy leaves. In this recipe, the chickpeas provide a chewiness that helps the taste linger longer.

20 MINUTES | SERVES **2** AS A MAIN, **4** AS A SIDE

INGREDIENTS
1 x 250 g pkt smoked rindless streaky bacon
2 handfuls of mixed salad leaves
1 large ripe tomato, halved and sliced into half moons
1 small red onion, peeled, halved and sliced into thin half moons
1 x 400 g can chickpeas, drained and rinsed
juice of ½ lemon
1 Tbsp olive oil
1 Tbsp mayonnaise
salt and freshly ground black pepper to taste

WHAT TO DO
1. Preheat the oven's grill. Separate the bacon and place the rashers on a baking tray. Grill for 7–10 minutes until crispy.
2. Place the salad leaves in a large mixing bowl, tearing the larger ones. Add the tomato, onion and chickpeas, and toss.
3. Mix the lemon juice, olive oil, mayonnaise, salt and pepper in a small jug and pour over the salad. Toss lightly.
4. Lastly, snip the still-warm crispy bacon into small bits and sprinkle over the salad.

> **TIP**   Adding cheese to this salad could make it too salty. If you have to have cheese, substitute the bacon for a smoked meat, like Parma ham.

LIGHT MEALS

CHICKEN SALAD

Being a student is all about ingenuity. Our lecturers tell us it's a great trait. Well, how about some ingenuity in the kitchen? Since I often make more than I need for one meal, like roasting a whole chicken in the oven instead of just a thigh or two, I end up with a lot of leftover chicken. This salad is a great way to use up leftovers and make a meal go a long way.

10 MINUTES | SERVES 1–2

INGREDIENTS
½ **lemon**
1 **shallot, cut into thin rings**
2 **spring onions, cut into thin rings (chop and set aside the green leaves)**
handful of rocket, shred larger leaves
1 **cup shredded cooked chicken (be sure to include pieces of crispy skin)**
olive oil
salt and freshly ground black pepper to taste
⅓ **cup sunflower or pumpkin seeds, toasted**

WHAT TO DO
1. Squeeze the lemon over the shallot and spring onion rings in a small mixing bowl – the lemon juice will slightly pickle the onion taste.
2. Arrange the rocket on your serving plate and top with the chicken.
3. Sprinkle over the onion rings with some of the lemon juice.
4. Dress the salad with olive oil and season with salt and pepper.
5. Lastly, scatter over the toasted seeds and serve.

> TIP   I sometimes add a dollop of mayonnaise or mustard to the lemon juice to sweeten the dish.

LIGHT MEALS

HONEY BEAN SALAD

Legumes are a great way to fulfil your daily nutrient needs, but they are often bland and boring. Why not try this salad next time you have a braai? It's so surprising that it may even be finished before the braai meat is ready!

10 MINUTES | SERVES **8** AS A SIDE

INGREDIENTS

1 large red onion, peeled, halved and sliced into very thin half moons
½ cup red wine vinegar
3 Tbsp honey
2 Tbsp olive oil
salt and freshly ground black pepper to taste
350 g green beans, topped and tailed
2 x 410 g cans butter beans
1 x 410 g can red kidney beans

WHAT TO DO

1. Place the onion in a mixing bowl and pour over the red wine vinegar. Add the honey and olive oil, and season to taste.
2. Bring a pot of salted water to the boil on the stove, add the green beans and blanch them for 2 minutes. Immediately pour out the boiling water and plunge the blanched beans into a bowl of iced water.
3. Drain and gently wash the butter and kidney beans with clean water.
4. Cut the green beans into thirds and place them in your serving bowl. Add the canned beans and the onion with its vinegar dressing.
5. Toss, cover and refrigerate. Remember to toss before serving.

> **TIP**   Stored in an airtight container, this salad will keep for about a week.

PROSCIUTTO SANDWICH

*Bread is a versatile foodstuff and the simple sandwich has hundreds of variations.
I went through a phase of smearing slices of bread with butter or mayonnaise and
using barbecue-flavour chips as a filling! This Italian-themed sandwich is, thankfully,
healthier and just as tasty!*

10 MINUTES | SERVES **1**

INGREDIENTS
knob of butter
2 large slices ciabatta bread
3 large slices mozzarella cheese
3–4 large, thin slices tomato
salt and freshly ground black pepper to taste
4–6 large basil leaves, finely chopped
2–3 slices prosciutto or parma ham
1 tsp honey

WHAT TO DO

1. Butter the bread slices on one side and turn them over.
2. On the unbuttered side of one, layer first a slice of cheese, followed by the
    slices of tomato. Season with salt and pepper and scatter over the basil. Layer
    another slice of cheese, pack on the prosciutto, drizzle over the honey and
    season with pepper. Add the last slice of cheese. Close the sandwich with the
    other slice of bread, leaving the buttered side on top, exposed.
3. Heat a frying pan on high. When hot, place the sandwich in it and press down
    gently with a spatula. Check after 1 minute to see if the bottom slice of bread
    has browned. If yes, turn over and press down gently until the middle slice of
    cheese has melted, and the other side of the sandwich has browned.
4. Serve warm or leave it to cool down before you wrap it in aluminium foil to
    eat on the go.

> TIP   This sandwich is great served with shoestring fries (long and thin chips).
> It makes the perfect snack for a hot summer's day, served with iced tea,
> alongside the pool.

HUMMUS TOASTIE

There is a great synergy between the earthy taste of hummus and the sweetness and saltiness of smoked meat. Try this when you are not in the mood to go all out and make a complicated toasted sandwich but are looking for something other than a PB&J. It's both yummy and filling!

5 MINUTES | SERVES **1**

INGREDIENTS
knob of butter
2 large slices wholewheat seeded bread
1 Tbsp hummus
salt and freshly ground black pepper to taste
2 large slices smoked beef
1 large gherkin, sliced lengthways
1 large lettuce leaf, stalk removed

WHAT TO DO
1. Butter each slice of bread on one side.
2. Smear the hummus on the unbuttered side of one slice. Season with salt and pepper and then add the smoked beef, gherkin and lettuce. Close the sandwich with the remaining slice of bread, the buttered side facing outwards.
3. Heat a frying pan on high. When very hot, lightly toast the sandwich on each side for 30 seconds at the most – just enough to form a crust but not to heat the hummus filling too much.

> **TIP** This also works well with rye bread and smoked or grilled bacon. For something different, try making this with my harissa hummus on page 53.

THE POWER SANDWICH

Sometimes a sandwich is all you want. If you eat them regularly, it's wise to bulk them up with protein and vitamins. This sandwich is packed with protein, while the spinach gives it a nutritious boost. It makes a hearty meal.

10 MINUTES | SERVES **1**

INGREDIENTS
1 egg
salt and freshly ground black pepper to taste
knob of butter
2 large slices rye bread
2 slices mature Cheddar cheese
3 rashers bacon, fried or grilled
handful of baby spinach leaves

WHAT TO DO
1. Fry the egg so that the yolk is still slightly runny (see page 17). Season with salt and pepper.
2. Butter the bread slices on one side and turn them over. On the unbuttered side of one, layer first a slice of cheese, followed by the rashers of bacon. Slide the egg on top and cover with a few spinach leaves. Add the last slice of cheese and close the sandwich with the remaining slice of bread, the buttered side facing outwards.
3. Heat a frying pan on high. When hot, place the sandwich in it and toast lightly for about 1 minute on each side.
4. Serve warm or cool it down before you wrap it in aluminium foil to eat on the go.

> TIP   Serve with a side salad or shoestring fries and some tomato sauce or onion marmalade (see page 50).

LIGHT MEALS

TOASTED BLT

Everyone loves a bacon, lettuce and tomato (BLT) sandwich. The addition of rye and some stringy white Gouda really makes this version stand out. The trick is to get the pan really hot so you don't cook the lettuce when toasting the sandwich, and to get the cheese to that point of 'just melted'.

15 MINUTES | SERVES **1**

INGREDIENTS
4 rashers bacon
knob of butter
2 large thin slices 100% rye bread or ciabatta
2 slices white Gouda cheese
4 lettuce leaves (Iceberg, butter or frilly), thick stalks removed
1 ripe tomato, sliced
salt and freshly ground black pepper to taste

WHAT TO DO
1. Preheat the oven's grill. Place the bacon rashers on a baking tray and grill for 5–7 minutes until crispy.
2. Butter the bread slices on one side and turn them over. On the unbuttered side of one, layer first a slice of cheese, followed by the bacon, lettuce and tomato. Season to taste, and then add the other slice of cheese. Close the sandwich with the remaining slice of bread, the buttered side facing outwards.
3. Heat a frying pan on high. When hot, lightly toast the sandwich, compressing it slightly with a spatula. After about 30 seconds, check to see how much it has browned – it mustn't burn. Turn off the heat and turn over the sandwich, compressing again for 40–60 seconds until the cheese softens or the bread browns nicely.

CHICKEN MAYONNAISE

A good chicken mayo recipe is hard to come by, and since there are often chicken leftovers in the fridge, it should be a staple in any novice kitchen. Here's my version.

30 MINUTES | SERVES **4**

INGREDIENTS

3 large chicken breasts, on the bone
salt and freshly ground black pepper to taste
1 lemon, halved
olive oil
3 Tbsp sweet and tangy mayonnaise (you can substitute half with
  cream cheese or smooth cottage cheese)
4 small spring onions, finely chopped
sprig of fresh tarragon, thyme or a few sage leaves, finely chopped

WHAT TO DO

1. Heat the oven to 200 °C. If your frying pan cannot go into the oven, warm a baking tray or casserole.
2. Season the chicken breasts with salt and pepper, and smear with the juice of one half of the lemon.
3. Heat some olive oil in a large frying pan on high and fry the chicken breasts for 3–5 minutes on each side until browned. They will still be raw on the inside.
4. Place the pan in the oven or transfer the chicken to the warmed baking tray or casserole. Cook for 10–15 minutes, then remove and allow to cool.
5. When the chicken has reached room temperature, remove the skin and bones, and finely shred the chicken meat.
6. Combine the chicken, mayonnaise, spring onions, herbs and some olive oil in a mixing bowl. Add the juice of the remaining lemon half and season to taste.

> **TIP** You can serve this on toast with some melted mozzarella, as a stand-alone meal, or as a meaty addition to a salad with some lettuce, chopped tomato and cucumber.

TUNA MAYONNAISE

Tuna mayonnaise is another fridge staple that you should get the hang of, not only because it's cheap but also because it's so nutritious!

5 MINUTES | SERVES **4**

INGREDIENTS
2 x 170 g cans shredded tuna in brine
2 Tbsp mayonnaise
1 small red onion, peeled and finely diced
juice of ½ lemon
1 Tbsp olive oil
1 heaped tsp finely grated ginger
½ tsp finely chopped green chilli
salt and freshly ground black pepper to taste

WHAT TO DO
1. Drain the tuna and place in a mixing bowl.
2. Add the remaining ingredients and mix thoroughly.

> **TIP** This is also great with some feta or blue cheese crumbled into it, and served on toast with cooked artichoke hearts. I often just add diced tomato and cucumber and eat it as a salad.

GUACAMOLE

I love my version of guacamole. Serve it as a (healthy) dip for party snacks or nachos, or mix some with tuna and finely sliced spring onion to use as a spread for toast. Alternatively, scoop into lettuce leaves for a quick salad.

5 MINUTES | SERVES **6** AS A DIP

INGREDIENTS
2 ripe avocados
1 Tbsp olive oil
1 Tbsp mayonnaise
1 Tbsp freshly squeezed lemon juice
salt and freshly ground black pepper to taste

WHAT TO DO
1. Slice each avocado in half lengthways and remove the pip. Using a spoon, scoop out the flesh and cube it. Place it in a bowl and mash with a fork.
2. Add the olive oil, mayonnaise and lemon juice, and mix thoroughly (but don't make a paste).
3. Season with salt and pepper, and serve.

> **TIP** Avocados can be hard and unripe when bought. Put them into a brown paper bag or newspaper to ripen. They are ripe when the skin gives way when a bit of pressure is applied. If not using a whole avo, slice it in half, smear the unused half with lemon juice and place, face down, on a plate to minimise contact with air (this will stop it from blackening).

LIGHT MEALS

ONION MARMALADE

This is an amazing condiment: spread it on toast, serve it with steak, or use as a sweet dip for party snacks.

ABOUT **1** HOUR | MAKES MULTIPLE SERVINGS — KEEPS WELL IN THE FRIDGE

INGREDIENTS
1 Tbsp butter
8–10 onions, peeled and thinly sliced or diced
about 5 fresh thyme stems
salt and freshly ground black pepper to taste
½ cup white wine
1½ cups brown or Demerara sugar
1 Tbsp balsamic glaze or vinegar
about 1 cup water

WHAT TO DO

1. Heat the butter in a large saucepan on medium heat and fry the onions for 5 minutes.
2. Add the thyme stems, season with salt and pepper, and turn the heat to high. When the temperature is noticeably warmer, add the wine.
3. Cook for 1 minute, stirring continuously. Reduce the heat back to medium and add the sugar, balsamic glaze or vinegar and a little water to help dissolve the sugar.
4. Cook for a further 20–30 minutes, adding a little water every now and then to prevent burning, until you get a sticky, marmalade-like consistency.
5. When the right consistency is reached, remove from the heat and pour into a sterilised glass jar.

HARISSA HUMMUS

Everyone seems to like hummus these days. It makes a great dip and sandwich spread, and is the perfect addition to a meze platter of crackers, cheese and preserved or smoked meats (for when you want to impress at a party). Here's my take on this healthy snack.

10 MINUTES | SERVES **2** AS A SPREAD, **6** AS A DIP

INGREDIENTS
1 x 400 g can chickpeas
¼ cup olive oil
1 Tbsp harissa paste
8 caraway seeds
salt and freshly ground black pepper to taste
1 Tbsp freshly squeezed lemon juice

WHAT TO DO
1. Drain the chickpeas and pulp them to a fine paste in a pestle and mortar or blender. Add half the olive oil and the harissa paste.
2. Grind the caraway seeds with some salt and pepper into a fine dust, and then add to the chickpea paste.
3. Now add the lemon juice and remaining olive oil. Mix thoroughly and serve.

> **TIP** For a more authentic taste, substitute 1 Tbsp ground cumin for the harissa. You can even add a little sugar to help sweeten the Mediterranean flavours. If you want to play around with something other than chickpeas, try this recipe with various types of canned beans or canned or soaked lentils. I usually have hummus on toast or crackers, or use it as a dip for carrot and cucumber sticks.

LIGHT MEALS

TAKING ON THE TAKEAWAY
WITH WRAPS, PIZZAS, BURGERS & PIES

People love takeaways! And why not? They taste so good. But have you ever tried making them at home? Burgers, wraps, pies, pizzas — these are all examples of takeaway foods. Why not try them out in your own kitchen — you may surprise yourself with how much cheaper it is in the long run, not to mention how much healthier!

WRAPS

When I discovered wraps in my second year, I was so enthusiastic about them that I immediately decided to host a dinner party at my flat, small as it was. Wraps sounded like minimal clean-up and, as it was summer, I figured they would go down well as a quick, cool dish. I casually announced my idea to a group of friends on the way to class one morning, my head brimming with ideas for fillings, but was met with stares of disbelief.

'No thanks,' one of them said. 'I'm not really into rap music, I hope you understand.'

Wraps are the new sandwiches. They taste delicious, allow for a greater variety of fillings, and there's even more than one way to wrap the wrap! Most of all, they are a welcome alternative to bread. You can even get low-GI, wheat-free and gluten-free wraps, so be assured there is a wrap out there for you.

Wraps are also incredibly versatile as you can basically 'wrap' anything. Here are a few suggestions, and a handy video link to show you how to wrap properly so as to keep your filling from falling out.

#breakfastwrapMunch

BREAKFAST WRAP

There are many ways to eat breakfast, but this must be my favourite – if you eat it correctly, you won't even need a knife and fork!

15 MINUTES | SERVES **1**

INGREDIENTS
scrambled egg for 1 (see page 16)
1 cheese-griller sausage
2–3 sundried tomatoes in olive oil (or soak your own)
1 tortilla wrap
sprig of fresh thyme, chopped

WHAT TO DO
1. Make the scrambled egg according to the recipe on page 16.
2. Heat the cheese-griller according to the packet instructions.
3. Snip the sundried tomatoes into quarters.
4. Place the wrap on a plate and pack the scrambled egg into the middle, spreading it out in a rectangular shape.
5. Place the sausage in the middle (there should be place for the wrap to fold at either end, otherwise cut the sausage to shorten it), and then scatter over the sundried tomatoes and thyme.
6. Fold over the left side, then the top and bottom, and lastly the right side of the wrap. Turn the wrap over so that the weight of the wrap seals the folds.
7. Heat a frying pan and quickly sear the wrap on both flat sides to seal it.

> **TIP** This also works well with bacon, and even smoked trout or snoek, as an alternative to the cheese-griller sausage.

SMOKED CHICKEN WRAP

This wrap tastes amazing with any smoked meat. Try it with a sweet Asian dressing, or a honey-mustard mayonnaise.

15 MINUTES | SERVES **1**

INGREDIENTS
1 tortilla wrap
1 Tbsp mayonnaise
handful of torn green leaves, such as a mixture of lettuce, rocket and basil
1 smoked chicken fillet, thinly sliced
dressing of your choice
4 cherry tomatoes, halved
salt and freshly ground black pepper to taste
handful of grated white Cheddar or Gouda cheese

WHAT TO DO
1. Place the wrap on a plate and smear the surface with the mayonnaise.
2. In the middle two-fifths of the wrap, layer the leaves and chicken. Drizzle over some dressing, and then layer the tomatoes on top and season to taste. Finally sprinkle over the cheese.
3. Fold over the left side, then the top and bottom, and lastly the right side of the wrap. Turn the wrap over so that the weight of the wrap seals the folds.
4. Heat a frying pan and quickly sear the wrap on both flat sides to seal it.
5. Slice diagonally and serve with a little olive oil, balsamic vinegar and honey.

> TIP You can really add anything to a wrap. Try bacon with Cheddar cheese, baby spinach and mushrooms fried in butter, or strips of quick-fried rare minute steak with honey and balsamic vinegar, butter lettuce and chopped spring onions. When making wraps to take away with you, wrap them in clingfilm — they make great, quick, work lunches or snacks for between classes.

TAKING ON THE TAKEAWAY

PIZZAS

Pizzas are synonymous with student life. Maybe it's because they go so well with beer (at a party) and milk (at home), or because there is nothing like a slice of pizza the morning after the night before. Pizza is always a winner, and when you learn to make these puppies yourself, you'll wonder why you spent so much of your money on expensive takeout with too much dough and too few toppings. Here is my fail-safe pizza base recipe, and a few ideas on how to go about topping your very own pizzas.

#pizzabasesMunch

PIZZA BASES

2–3 HOURS | MAKES 4

INGREDIENTS
500 g strong white bread flour
½ tsp salt
½ tsp sugar
10 g pkt instant dried yeast
½ cup olive oil blend (equal parts sunflower and olive oil, or any cooking oil)
2 cups lukewarm water
2 heaped tsp full-fat smooth cottage cheese

WHAT TO DO
1. Sift all the dry ingredients into a large mixing bowl.
2. Make a well in the centre about halfway through to the bottom of the bowl and pour in all the oil and half the water. Add the cottage cheese and mix with a wooden spoon to form a workable dough, on the verge of being sticky (add more water if necessary).
3. Turn the dough out onto a work surface and knead for about 5 minutes. Form the dough into a ball and place it in a mixing bowl. Cover the bowl with clingfilm and allow the dough to rest in a warm place until it has more than doubled in size. Knead once more and let it rise again until doubled in size.
4. Preheat the oven to 200 °C.
5. Divide the dough into 4 and roll out each portion into a round pizza base as thin as possible. You can fold over the edges if you want thicker sides. Depending on the size of your baking tray, you can make square or oval pizzas too.
6. Place the bases on baking trays and bake each for 10 minutes.
7. Allow the bases to cool before freezing for later, or add toppings and make the pizzas immediately.

MEDITERRANEAN PIZZA

This pizza is so simple to make. The flavours conjure images of islands, sea and sun.

15–20 MINUTES | MAKES 2

INGREDIENTS
1 x 115 g can tomato paste
2 Tbsp olive oil
freshly ground black pepper to taste
2 homemade pizza bases, precooked
300 g mozzarella cheese, coarsely grated
bunch of basil leaves, half shredded and half left whole
4 large fresh tomatoes, thinly sliced
12 slices sweet and peppery salami, quartered
1 cup pitted black olives, sliced in half lengthways

WHAT TO DO
1. Preheat the oven to 180 °C.
2. Mix the tomato paste, olive oil and some pepper and smear over the pizza bases. Sprinkle over half the cheese.
3. Top with the shredded basil, followed by the tomato, salami and olives. Cover with the whole basil leaves and sprinkle over the remaining cheese.
4. Bake the pizzas for a few minutes just until the cheese melts.

> TIP   Using pesto as a spread on pizza bases is gaining in popularity. Why not make your own pesto? You can also use it as a spaghetti topping with mushrooms and chicken.

TAKING ON THE TAKEAWAY

BOEREWORS PIZZA

*I cooked up this pizza when I didn't have all the standard pizza toppings in my fridge.
It turned out surprisingly good! Cook some extra boerewors when you have a braai and use
it for making pizza the next night.*

30 MINUTES | MAKES **2**

INGREDIENTS
400–500 g thin boerewors
1 x 115 g can tomato paste
2 Tbsp olive oil
1 Tbsp finely chopped fresh rosemary
2 homemade pizza bases, precooked
200 g white Gouda cheese, coarsely grated
salt and freshly ground black pepper to taste
15–20 cherry tomatoes, halved

WHAT TO DO

1. Preheat the oven to 180 °C.
2. If you are using fresh boerewors, fry it in a frying pan and set to one side.
   When cool enough to handle, slice into 2cm-thick rounds.
3. Mix the tomato paste with the olive oil and rosemary, and smear over the
   pizza bases. Sprinkle over half the cheese.
4. Top with the boerewors slices and cherry tomatoes, and season with salt
   and pepper. Sprinkle over the remaining cheese, garnish with a little extra
   rosemary and bake for 10 minutes.

> **TIP** You can add whatever toppings you want to your pizzas — it's all about
> personal taste. Mushrooms work well in this recipe.

BURGERS

We all love burgers – they're cool, they're fast and most of all, they taste good. Make your own burgers at home and see if you can beat the taste of your local takeout.

#burgerpattiesMunch

BURGER PATTIES

Try to make your own beef burger patties when you can. This is a great recipe. If you are willing to spend a little extra to get the best burger possible, ask the butcher to finely mince 2–3 aged sirloin steaks for you.

80 MINUTES | SERVES 6–8

INGREDIENTS
500 g lean beef mince
½ cup breadcrumbs
1 small onion, peeled and finely grated and squeezed of excess juice
½ tsp finely chopped fresh thyme
½ tsp finely chopped fresh parsley
1 Tbsp soy sauce
1 tsp freshly ground black pepper
1 egg
8 caraway seeds, finely crushed in a pestle and mortar with a pinch of salt
2 Tbsp olive oil

WHAT TO DO

1. Combine everything in a large mixing bowl and form into patties no more than 3 cm thick. Make them as wide as the buns you want to serve them on. Rest the mixture in the fridge for at least an hour.
2. Heat a large frying pan and fry the patties for about 4 minutes on each side until nicely browned. Don't press down on the patties, otherwise the juices will run out. Remove them from the heat and allow them to rest.

> **TIP** Why not make a burger pie for when you really need it after a good night out? Seal a cooked patty and a slice of cheese in some puff pastry. Wrap the pie in aluminium foil and freeze for when you're in the mood. Defrost in the fridge and then bake in a 200ºC oven for about 20 minutes.

TAKING ON THE TAKEAWAY

ALTERNATE BURGER PATTIES

This makes a delicious burger too.

80 MINUTES | SERVES **6–8**

INGREDIENTS
1 slice rye bread
1 egg
500 g extra-lean beef mince
2 Tbsp sundried tomato paste
1 Tbsp olive oil
1 onion, peeled and finely diced
sprig of fresh thyme, finely chopped
salt and freshly ground black pepper to taste

WHAT TO DO
1. Mash the bread into the egg and set aside.
2. Combine the mince and the remaining ingredients in a large mixing bowl. Add the mashed bread and mix thoroughly.
3. Form the mixture into patties no more than 3 cm thick. Make them as wide as the buns you want to serve them on. Rest in the fridge for at least an hour.
4. Heat a large frying pan and fry the patties for about 4 minutes on each side until nicely browned. Don't press down on the patties, otherwise the juices will run out. Remove them from the heat and allow them to rest.

TAKING ON THE TAKEAWAY

BALSAMIC BURGERS

These are delicious and a sure way to liven up a party! Make the burger patties according to the recipe on page 62.

10 MINUTES | SERVES **4**

INGREDIENTS
4 homemade burger patties
¼ cup balsamic reduction, or 2 tsp brown sugar dissolved in
   ¼ cup balsamic vinegar
4 round buns, halved and buttered
8 butter lettuce leaves
8 slices mature Cheddar cheese
1 large tomato, thickly sliced
2 gherkins, thinly sliced lengthways
4 tsp onion marmalade (see page 50)

WHAT TO DO
1. Cook the patties for about four minutes a side. In the last 2 minutes, add the balsamic reduction or vinegar mixture to the pan. It should glaze the patties and provide a bit of a sauce for the burgers. Set aside to rest while you assemble your burger.
2. Build your burger on a bun as follows: 1 lettuce leaf, 2 slices of cheese, gherkin slices, burger patty, a drizzle of balsamic glaze, 1 tomato slice, 1 lettuce leaf, 1 tsp onion marmalade.
3. Serve with chips (see page 67) or North African couscous (see page 33).

TAKING ON THE TAKEAWAY

CHICKEN BURGERS

Chicken is much cheaper than mince, so people often opt for this kind of burger to make at home. My recipe is great for when you are home alone or when you are catering for a party. Either way you'll be having a blast after trying these!

30 MINUTES | SERVES **4**

INGREDIENTS
1 lemon, halved
4 chicken fillets, butterflied
salt and freshly ground black pepper to taste
olive oil
½ cup mayonnaise
1 Tbsp mustard
1 small red chilli, finely diced
4 round sesame seed buns, halved and buttered
about 8 frilly lettuce leaves
4 thick slices white Cheddar cheese
1 large ripe tomato, thickly sliced

WHAT TO DO
1. Squeeze the juice of half a lemon over the chicken fillets, season with salt and pepper and drizzle over some olive oil. Rub the fillets so that they are evenly coated.
2. Heat some more olive oil in a frying pan on high and fry the chicken fillets for 3 minutes on each side.
3. Make a sauce by combining the mayonnaise, mustard, chilli and juice of the remaining lemon half.
4. Build your burger on a bun as follows: 1 lettuce leaf, a drizzle of sauce, ½ chicken fillet, 1 cheese slice, 1 tomato slice, salt and pepper to taste, ½ chicken fillet (optional), 1 lettuce leaf.

> **TIP** This makes a great filling for a wrap as well!

TAKING ON THE TAKEAWAY

CHIPS

South Africans call them slap tjips, *Americans call them French fries and the French call them* pommes frites. *Whatever you want to call them, no burger meal is complete without a healthy portion of fries. This is my 'healthier' version, but it sure doesn't skimp on taste!*

1 HOUR | SERVES 2–4

INGREDIENTS
6–8 large potatoes, washed (Yukon is a great variety for making chips, as is Mediterranean-style)
non-stick cooking spray
⅓ cup olive oil
1 Tbsp fresh rosemary leaves
1 Tbsp coarse sea salt

WHAT TO DO
1. Boil the potatoes (in their skins) in a pot of salted water for about 10–15 minutes. Drain and leave to dry.
2. Preheat the oven to 200 °C. Grease a baking tray with non-stick cooking spray.
3. When the potatoes have cooled enough to handle, slice them into chips and place in a mixing bowl. Pour in the olive oil and mix gently to evenly coat the chips.
4. Evenly spread out the chips on the baking tray and bake for 25–30 minutes until they start to brown. Remove the tray from the oven and, with a spatula, carefully mix the chips so that most of the sides that have been on the tray are now on top.
5. Increase the oven's temperature to 220 °C and bake for a further 5–10 minutes, or until the chips are the desired colour.
6. Grind the rosemary and salt in a pestle and mortar to a fine green dust. Sprinkle over the chips and serve.

> **TIP** These chips are amazing! Leaving the skins on the potatoes gives them a real, earthy taste. Try parsnips and sweet potatoes too, and experiment with different herb salts.

TAKING ON THE TAKEAWAY

PIES

So we all know pies are calorie bombs, but sometimes you just get that craving for a proper pie, something with a doughy crust and warm filling. Here are a few ideas you can try at home.

SPINACH PIES

This amazing pie is based on the Greek spanakopita filling – like a samosa with spinach and feta cheese. Only this one is a bit better!

30–35 MINUTES | SERVES 6

INGREDIENTS
1 x 400 g roll puff pastry, defrosted in the fridge
large bunch of spinach, destemmed and finely shredded
2 wheels feta cheese, crumbled
2 eggs, lightly beaten
5 sprigs fresh rosemary, finely chopped

WHAT TO DO
1. Preheat the oven to 180 °C. Grease a baking tray.
2. Roll out the puff pastry into a rectangular shape large enough to fit your baking tray. Slice 2 cm-thick lengths off each side and add to the new rectangular-shaped pastry, building 'walls'.
3. Wilt the spinach in a pot of salted water for about 2 minutes until soft. Drain and mix with the feta and eggs. Spoon the filling into the pastry shell and sprinkle the rosemary over the top.
4. Bake for 20–25 minutes until golden and serve with onion marmalade (see page 50).

> **TIP** As a variation, try an onion marmalade and bacon filling.

TAKING ON THE TAKEAWAY

CHEESE-GRILLER PIES

This is my take on the infamous pie associated with students all over South Africa. I think you'll find this version much tastier, and cheaper in the long run!

30–35 MINUTES | MAKES **8**

INGREDIENTS
1 x 400 g roll puff pastry, defrosted in the fridge
8 cheese-griller sausages
100 g Cheddar cheese, coarsely grated
1 egg, whisked with 1 Tbsp milk
¼ cup sesame seeds

WHAT TO DO
1. Preheat the oven to 200 °C. Grease a baking tray.
2. Gently roll out the puff pastry until it increases in size by about 5 cm in each direction (in a rectangular shape).
3. Lay the cheese-grillers in a 2 x 4 grid so that you can gauge how much pastry you still need to roll out. Then cut out the pastry rectangles for each pie.
4. Position a cheese-griller running lengthways in the middle of each rectangle and sprinkle over some cheese. Wet the edges of the rectangles with water and fold the pastry over the filling. Press down to seal the edges.
5. Trim off any excess pastry and place the pies on the baking tray. Brush with the egg mixture, sprinkle some sesame seeds on top and make small diagonal slits in the pastry (but don't cut through it).
6. Bake for 20–25 minutes or until golden.

> **TIP** You can use any kind of sausage (viennas, brockwurst, etc.) – once you start getting the hang of using pastry, you'll start coming up with other ideas on how to use it! You can also use brown bread flour puff pastry, but don't roll it out too thinly as it tends to break more easily.

TAKING ON THE TAKEAWAY

DON'T BE CHICKEN
– COOK CHICKEN!

Let's face it: chicken is probably the meat that most people use for mealtimes. This used to fill me with dread, because I held the opinion that chicken (and minced meat) is the blandest, most boring meat you can find. I'll have you know that I've since changed my chicken-hating ways. Not only is chicken the cheapest meat you can buy, it's also one of the most flexible when it comes to how it can be cooked.

Whole chickens make amazing one-pot dishes – and don't be afraid of eating meat off the bone: the flavours of a whole chicken cooked to perfection compare favourably to chicken fillets, which tend to be both dry and – you guessed it – bland. (Chicken fillets do have their place, though – chopped up they make wonderful stir-fries and pasta dishes.) Drumsticks and wings are great for soaking up sweet and spicy marinades, and are delicious done either in the oven or on the braai. And let's not forget the thighs – brown chicken meat is not only tastier and more succulent, but it also lends itself to a wider variety of uses – deboned and filled, stewed or casseroled, or marinated and braaied.

Here are a few recipes that not only show you the versatility of chicken, but also show you that in fact it is the most amazing vehicle for flavours – who knew being bland could have such an upside?

ASIAN CHICKEN SWEETCORN SOUP

One of my favourite things about making roast chicken is the abundance of things I can do with the leftover meat. On a day that ends with a slight chill – think autumn – this soup is especially delicious.

ABOUT **30** MINUTES | SERVES **2–4**

INGREDIENTS
1 cup leftover shredded chicken
1 x 415 g can creamstyle sweetcorn
4 cups warm water
1 tsp chicken stock powder or ½ cube
soy sauce and white pepper to taste
2 tsp cornflour
1 egg white, whisked

WHAT TO DO
1. Put the chicken, sweetcorn, water and chicken stock in a pot. Bring to the boil and then turn down the heat to medium to maintain a simmer.
2. Simmer for 20 minutes and then add soy sauce and white pepper to taste.
3. Scoop out ½ cup of liquid, mix in the cornflour and add back to the soup, bit by bit until the desired consistency is reached.
4. After another 5 minutes, slowly add the egg white in a long thin stream, and stir gently. The egg white should make thin white stripes in the soup. This is a typically Asian method of making soup. The egg white adds protein and also acts as a sieve to help clarify the soup.
5. Serve as is.

> **TIP**   If you haven't got leftover chicken, just fry a large chicken breast on the bone until cooked and tear it into fine shreds with a knife and fork. You can also add thin egg noodles if you like.

DON'T BE CHICKEN

CHICKEN & LEMON CASSEROLE

This dish made me realise that chicken can taste good, and led me to experiment more with this versatile bird. It's a one-pot dinner for one (the leftovers keep really well) or serves up to four people. The great thing about this dish is that if you have everything else, you can even add a second chicken, if there is space for it in your casserole — very economical if you are planning to make a soup or pie from the leftover meat and vegetables the next day.

TAKES SOME TIME | SERVES **4**

INGREDIENTS
1 whole chicken
4 potatoes, peeled and quartered
3 onions, peeled and quartered
several large cloves garlic, unpeeled
6–10 medium Roma tomatoes, halved lengthways
2 medium lemons, halved
3 sprigs each of fresh rosemary and thyme
salt and freshly ground black pepper to taste
2 Tbsp olive oil

WHAT TO DO
1. Preheat the oven to 200 °C.
2. Trim the chicken of any excess fat, remove the extra skin at the neck and place in the middle of the casserole. Pack the potatoes, onions, garlic and tomatoes around it. Squeeze lemon juice over everything and place the squeezed halves around the chicken.
3. Strip the leaves from the rosemary and thyme sprigs and scatter them over the casserole. Season well with salt and pepper and drizzle over the olive oil. Cover the casserole with its lid.
4. Cook for 1 hour, then remove the lid and baste the chicken with some of the juices that have collected at the bottom of the dish. Increase the temperature to 220 °C and return the casserole to the oven, leaving the lid ajar, for about 20 minutes until the chicken skin is golden and crispy.
5. Remove the dish from the oven and let it rest for 10 minutes before serving.

> TIP If I make this for myself, I eat the drumsticks and thighs and leave the breast meat for either pie filling (with the leftover sauce, onions and potatoes) or chicken mayonnaise the next day — check out my recipe on page 48.

CHICKEN SCHNITZEL

I grew up loving pork schnitzel – until I discovered you can do it with chicken too! This dish is a great favourite amongst my friends, so it would be remiss not to include it here!

45 MINUTES | SERVES 2

INGREDIENTS
2 large deboned chicken breasts
50 ml buttermilk
50 g fine breadcrumbs
1 Tbsp cornflour
salt and freshly ground black pepper to taste
1 Tbsp sunflower oil
1 Tbsp butter

WHAT TO DO
1. Butterfly the chicken breasts and flatten them a bit with a meat mallet or dough roller.
2. Place the chicken breasts in a shallow dish and cover with the buttermilk. Set aside for about 30 minutes to allow them to soften.
3. Mix the breadcrumbs with the cornflour, and season with salt and pepper. Spread the mixture on a plate and coat the chicken fillets (pat gently to make sure the coating sticks and covers the entire fillet).
4. Heat the sunflower oil in a frying pan. When it just about starts smoking, add the butter and when it melts, immediately mix it with the oil and add the schnitzels.
5. Fry for about 2 minutes on each side or until golden. Rest the schnitzels on paper towel for a minute to allow the excess oil to drain.
6. Serve with a simple lettuce, tomato and onion salad, or homemade potato wedges.

> **TIP** To butterfly chicken breasts, cut horizontally through the thickest part of the breast, taking care not to cut all the way through. Open out, and flatten by patting down firmly with the palm of your hand.

BEER CHICKEN

If you have ever had chicken cooked in beer you will know that beer imparts an amazing flavour to the meat. This one-pot dish is a variation of the one I grew up with. It goes very well with rice or slices of lightly buttered baguette (French loaf). As with most one-pot dishes, you can double the recipe, provided your pot is big enough to take the load. Add about 15 minutes at the most onto the cooking time.

TAKES SOME TIME | SERVES **4**

INGREDIENTS

3 heaped tsp chicken stock powder or 2 cubes
2 tsp garam masala
1 tsp ground cumin
2 bottles beer (I usually use Windhoek Lager)
1 whole chicken or 8 thighs
4 medium potatoes, peeled and quartered
3 large onions, peeled and quartered
1 tsp freshly ground black pepper
2 sprigs of fresh thyme, chopped
salt, freshly ground black pepper and brown sugar to taste
1 cup fresh cream

WHAT TO DO

1. Dissolve the chicken stock powder, garam masala and ground cumin in 2 cups (500ml) beer. Drink the rest of the beer while cooking!
2. Place the chicken in a potjie or stockpot. Arrange the potatoes and onions around it and pour over the beer stock. Sprinkle over the pepper and thyme.
3. Simmer on medium-low heat, or cook in the oven at 180°C, for about 1 hour.
4. After about an hour, increase the heat a little and taste the sauce. Season with salt and pepper if needs be, or even a little brown sugar if you prefer a sweeter dish. Now add three-quarters of the cream and stir gently for 10 minutes. Taste the sauce again and decide if you need more cream (if it is too thin or too salty, you will need to add more).
5. Simmer for another 15 minutes on medium-low heat until the sauce thickens enough to serve.

> **TIP** If I make this for myself, I keep the sauce, vegetables and remaining deboned meat to use as a pie filling the next day. You can make individual pies and freeze them.

DON'T BE CHICKEN

ASIAN-STYLE CHICKEN STIR-FRY

Who doesn't love eating a dish with chopsticks? This is a great way to make chicken fun and fast! And it's perfect for leftovers the following day as the noodles soak up the sauce.

QUICK | SERVES **2–3**

INGREDIENTS
4 chicken breasts, skinned and deboned
handful of spring onions, chopped or 1 large red onion, peeled
handful of green beans
handful of broccoli florets
handful of cauliflower florets
2–3 large carrots, peeled and julienned
3 bricks egg noodles (they are usually sold in packets of 6)
vegetable oil
2 cloves garlic, peeled and chopped
1 green or red chilli, deseeded and finely chopped
about 1 tsp grated fresh ginger
1 Tbsp brown sugar dissolved in 2 Tbsp soy sauce
1 tsp freshly ground black pepper

WHAT TO DO
1. Cut the chicken breasts into strips across the breadth of the fillet (if you cut lengthways, the meat won't be as tender).
2. If using a whole onion, halve and then finely slice it to make half-moons. Top and tail the green beans, and cut them into thirds. Cut the broccoli and cauliflower into mini florets about the size of a teaspoon.
3. Place the onions, beans and carrots in a microwavable container and microwave on high for 3 minutes. Now add the broccoli and cauliflower and microwave again for 2 minutes.
4. Bring a pot of salted water to the boil and cook the egg noodles for 3 minutes. Drain and set aside.
5. Now comes the quick part: heat some vegetable oil in a very hot frying pan or wok. Fry the garlic, chilli and ginger for a few seconds, and then add the chicken strips. Brown for about 1 minute, and then add the soy sauce and brown sugar for a further minute. Add the pepper and toss to coat.
6. Now add the cooked noodles and vegetables. Turn off the heat and stir-fry on the residual heat for 1 minute, tossing continuously to get the sauce evenly distributed.
7. Eat immediately. If there are any leftovers, allow to cool, toss again and refrigerate in a plastic container. You can even freeze it – although you'll sacrifice some crunch.

> **TIP** If you want to sweeten the dish even more, add about 1 cup chopped pineapple. Try this recipe with pork strips instead of chicken.

DON'T BE CHICKEN

PRAWN CHICKEN ROLLS

I got the idea for this after I had a similar dish in Namibia. It takes a bit of preparation, but not too much really, if you consider what you're getting out of it. Keep this for when you invite that special someone over.

45 MINUTES | SERVES **2–4**

INGREDIENTS
4 chicken breast fillets, butterflied (see page 77)
salt and freshly ground black pepper to taste
8 prawns (deveined, peeled and ready-cooked)
1 Tbsp olive oil
1 tsp paprika
olive oil for frying
butter
1 x 410 g can dessert peach slices in syrup
1 tsp crushed Madagascar green peppercorns
1 tsp whole Madagascar green peppercorns
1 cup fresh cream

WHAT TO DO
1. Season the chicken with salt and pepper.
2. Coat the prawns in the 1 Tbsp olive oil and paprika. Fill the chicken fillets with 2 prawns each. Secure the chicken rolls with string or toothpicks to ensure the prawns stay inside and the rolls retain their shape.
3. Heat some olive oil and butter in a frying pan on high and sear the chicken rolls for about 2 minutes on each side. Set the rolls aside and remove the toothpicks or string – they should keep their shape.
4. Chop the peaches and add them and their syrup to the pan you used to fry the chicken.
5. Add the crushed and whole peppercorns and three-quarters of the cream (if you like a creamier sauce, add the rest). Reduce the sauce for about 7 minutes on medium-high heat, before adding the chicken rolls. Simmer for another 5 minutes, or until the sauce reaches the desired consistency.
6. Serve on a bed of brown basmati rice, with lots of sauce spooned over – it's delicious!

> **TIP**   You can substitute the prawns with 100 g blanched, deveined shrimp.

DON'T BE CHICKEN

CHICKEN LIVER PASTA

Chicken livers are a cheap source of protein but are often regarded with a slight raise of the eyebrow. That is until you try this recipe! It's great for a night in watching a few episodes of your favourite series.

ABOUT **30** MINUTES | SERVES **2**

INGREDIENTS
about **500 g** chicken livers, rinsed and dried
1 Tbsp butter
sprig of fresh thyme, chopped
salt and freshly ground black pepper to taste
1 x 500 g pkt penne pasta
olive oil
1 tsp chopped fresh garlic
1 cup sundried tomato mix (chop **3–4** sundried tomatoes
   and mix with **2 x 115 g** cans tomato paste)
1 cup cream
pinch of cayenne pepper or dried chilli flakes

WHAT TO DO
1. Carefully clean the chicken livers by cutting out any bits of sinew or clotted blood without tearing them.
2. Melt the butter in a medium-hot frying pan. Add the thyme and chicken livers, and stir gently to coat for about 1 minute. Season with salt and pepper and place in a small mixing bowl.
3. Start cooking the penne according to the packet instructions.
4. Heat some olive oil in the pan you used for the chicken livers. Fry the garlic for 1 minute.
5. Add the sundried tomato mush, stir for 1 minute, and then add the cream. Bring to a slight simmer before adding the cayenne pepper or chilli flakes. Simmer for 5 minutes.
6. Remove the pan from the heat, add the chicken livers and allow them to rest for about 2 minutes.
7. By now the pasta should be about done (you want it to have a slight bite to it – called *al dente*). Drain the pasta and toss with the chicken livers. Serve with a sprinkling of thyme and black pepper.

> **TIP** Up the ante and serve with some Parmesan or Pecorino cheese grated over it.

DURBAN CHICKEN CURRY WITH HOMEMADE ROTIS

I love this curry because it's so easy. I like to make my own rotis and eat it with my hands!

50 MINUTES | SERVES **4**

INGREDIENTS
1½ cups cake flour
½ cup warm water
pinch of salt
sunflower oil
2 medium potatoes, peeled and diced
2 medium onions, peeled and diced
3–4 tsp Durban curry spice mix, or a pre-prepared paste
   (add more if you are adventurous!)
4 chicken breasts, cubed
1 Tbsp butter
2 x 410 g cans tomato purée
1 cup full-fat Bulgarian yoghurt
extra spices to taste
2 tsp brown sugar

WHAT TO DO
1. Mix the flour, water and salt to form a dough – add more water if the dough is too dry (a little at a time). Leave to rest until the curry is almost done.
2. Heat 2 Tbsp sunflower oil in a large saucepan and fry the potatoes, onions and curry spice over medium heat for 5–7 minutes.
3. Add the chicken and butter and fry for 2 minutes – add more butter if the pan gets sticky.
4. Add the first can of tomato purée and the yoghurt. Simmer for about 5 minutes, stirring continuously. Add more tomato purée and extra spices at your discretion, depending on how creamy you want the sauce. Add the brown sugar. Turn to the lowest heat level and simmer slowly for at least 40 minutes to allow the spices and flavour to develop.
5. Divide the dough into 6 balls. Use your hands to flatten each ball into a circle then roll it out so it just barely fits into your largest frying pan. Make the dough as thin as possible, without tearing it.
6. Heat 1 tsp sunflower oil in the pan over a very high heat and then add a roti. Smear the leftover oil on the teaspoon over the surface of the roti. It should puff up a little bit.
7. Cook for about 1 minute and then turn over to cook the other side. The roti should be nicely browned but not burnt. Keep the cooked rotis warm and moist in a container with a lid as you cook the rest.
8. Serve the curry with the rotis. For an authentic experience, tear the rotis into pieces and use these to scoop up the curry with your hands.

> **TIP** To highlight the spices and soothe the tongue, serve with cooling sambals like a chopped tomato and mango salsa or pickled beetroot.

DON'T BE CHICKEN

CATCH OF THE DAY

& SOME OTHER FISHY BITES

We are a nation of meat eaters. I recently heard British chef Gordon Ramsay mention, in an almost shocked tone, that the French eat 90 kg meat per person per year. I thought '... *hmmm that sounds about right'*. But we enjoy our fish, too.

South Africa is blessed with a vast coastline, and lots of value-for-money seafood awaits the curious and patient grocery shopper. For young people, fish and seafood is not only a cheaper alternative to meats like lamb, it is also quick and easy to prepare. Plus it's so healthy! If you can manage it, try having fish or seafood at least once a week. (That tin of tuna you mixed with mayo when you got home from gym or class doesn't count, although keep at it!)

What follows are a few seafood dishes I made when I was a student. It took me a while to warm up to cooking seafood on a regular basis, but the variation in flavours, the availability of fresh catches, as well as the pricing made it almost a necessity. Now I make a seafood dish at least once a week – and I love it!

The proper management of fish and seafood harvested for human consumption should always be on your mind. Visit the Southern African Sustainable Seafood Initiative (SASSI) website (www.wwfsassi.co.za) and insist on buying only responsibly caught, sustainable fish and seafood from your grocer or fishmonger – it's your right as a paying customer!

BRAAI PRAWNS

Yes, it feels weird to braai seafood — especially considering the abundance of red meat in our country. The Australians love using coals and flames to bring out the best in seafood. Follow their lead and make this as a starter so that everyone has something to munch on before the main event is braaied.

40 MINUTES | SERVES 4–6

INGREDIENTS
24 deveined prawns, defrosted if frozen
2 Tbsp olive oil
1 tsp smoked paprika
½ tsp salt
½ tsp freshly ground black pepper
sprig of fresh rosemary, chopped
1 whole lemon, halved
8 wooden skewers, soaked in water for 30 minutes

WHAT TO DO
1. Place the prawns in a large mixing bowl and drizzle over the oil, paprika, salt, pepper, rosemary and juice of half a lemon. Mix gently.
2. Marinate the prawns for at least 30 minutes before braaiing.
3. Make sure the coals or flames are at a medium-high heat. Thread 3 prawns onto each skewer. Braai the prawns for no more than 2 minutes per side, squeezing over the remaining lemon juice before turning them. Use a hinged grill so you don't have to worry about turning each skewer individually. If using an open grid, take it off the heat so you don't burn yourself.
4. Serve with guacamole (see page 49), harissa-flavoured hummus (see page 53) or homemade tartare sauce (see page 103).

> TIP Defrost frozen prawns in the fridge for a few hours. Defrosting too quickly or using the microwave will turn the prawn meat to mush.
> If making a fire is too much of a schlep, you can grill the prawn kebabs for 5 minutes a side in the oven.
> Try this marinade with calamari tubes or steaks (remember to score the steaks to stop them curling) or baby squid. For extra bite, I like to add some cayenne pepper or chilli flakes!

FRESH FISH

Here is a failsafe recipe you can use to cook a variety of fish, including geelbek, red roman, angelfish, John (Cape) Dory, kingklip and kabeljou (kob). Most of these are on SASSI's 'orange' list (see page 89), which means you should only enjoy them every now and then.

35 MINUTES | SERVES 2

INGREDIENTS
3 beetroot, washed, peeled and quartered
2 turnips or 5 radishes, washed, peeled and diced
1 Tbsp brown or treacle sugar
3 tsp chopped fresh thyme
3 Tbsp olive oil
salt and freshly ground black pepper to taste
1 large fresh fish fillet, halved
soft butter
½ lemon

WHAT TO DO
1. Preheat the oven to 220 °C.
2. Toss the beetroot and turnips or radishes in the sugar, 1 tsp chopped thyme, 2 Tbsp olive oil and salt to taste.
3. Place the vegetables on a baking tray, spacing them out evenly, and bake for 45–60 minutes, depending on the size of the vegetables. They should be crisp on the outside and soft on the inside.
4. When the vegetables have about 10 minutes to go, rub the fish with some soft butter and season with salt and pepper and the leftover thyme.
5. Heat the remaining olive oil in a large frying pan over high heat and fry the fish, skin side down, for about 30 seconds before turning the heat down to medium. Cook for 2 minutes before carefully turning over the fish with a spatula. Squeeze over the lemon and after 3 minutes, turn the fish again. Baste the flesh with the pan juices, turn off the heat and serve with the crispy vegetables.

> **TIP** For a variation, use whatever vegetables you like, such as onions and potatoes, or green peppers and cherry tomatoes, depending on your taste.

HOMEMADE FISH 'N CHIPS

You can use any white, flaky fish for this, not just hake! Ask the fishmonger what is fresh, and get them to debone and fillet it for you. Frozen hake is fine, but it would be a shame to use the frozen stuff if you are able to buy fresh. Remember to let frozen fish defrost in the fridge – never defrost it in the microwave.

40 MINUTES | SERVES **2**

INGREDIENTS
6 medium potatoes, washed but not peeled
non-stick cooking spray
olive oil
2 Tbsp cornflour
2 Tbsp all-purpose flour
1 egg
1 cup beer (I like Windhoek Draught)
chopped fresh chives or dill to taste
salt and freshly ground black pepper to taste
sunflower oil
2 medium hake fillets, skinned and deboned
1 lemon, quartered

WHAT TO DO
1. Boil the potatoes in a pot of salted water for 5–7 minutes. Drain and leave to cool until manageable.
2. Preheat the oven to 200 °C. Grease a baking tray with non-stick cooking spray.
3. Leaving the skins on, cut the potatoes into chips and toss them in just enough olive oil to coat them. Evenly space the chips on the baking tray and bake for 35 minutes or until golden and crispy.
4. Combine the cornflour, flour, egg, beer and a sprinkling of chives or dill in a mixing bowl. Season with salt and pepper and tip into a rectangular container large enough to hold the fish fillets.
5. Heat a large frying pan on the highest setting and add enough sunflower oil to comfortably cover the base of the pan.
6. When the oil is hot and almost smoking, take a fish fillet by the tail and dip it into the batter on both sides and immediately put it in the pan.
7. Cook for 1–2 minutes, but only turn when the crust turns golden. Turn the fish using a spatula and cook for 2–3 minutes on the other side. Take it out of the pain and drain on a paper towel while you cook the other fillet. Resting the fish allows the residual heat to cook it all the way through.
8. When the chips are done and the fish is on the plate, quickly grind the remaining dill with some salt and sprinkle over the chips. Serve with a quarter or two of lemon and some tomato sauce mixed with mayonnaise.

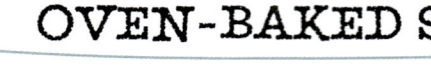

OVEN-BAKED SNOEK

Snoek is plentiful at certain times of the year, making it a cheap and viable meal. I got this recipe from my dad, and it also works well with yellowtail. If you buy pre-packed snoek from the supermarket, it doesn't need to be salted.

OVER AN HOUR | SERVES **4–5**

INGREDIENTS
1 cup coarse-ground (rock) salt
1 medium fresh snoek, butterflied
1 Tbsp butter
2 lemons
1 heaped tsp crushed garlic
½ cup apricot jam
⅓ cup (±80g) butter
1 tsp freshly ground black pepper

WHAT TO DO
1. Pour about 1 cup salt over the snoek and leave it for 20–30 minutes. Wash off the salt under running water for about 3 minutes. Pat dry. If using frozen snoek, defrost it slowly before salt-washing it. The snoek is now ready to be cooked.
2. Preheat the oven to 180 °C.
3. Smear a baking tray with 1 Tbsp butter and lay the snoek onto it, skin side down. Squeeze over the juice of 1 lemon and evenly scatter over the garlic.
4. Melt the apricot jam and ⅓ cup butter in a small saucepan. Add the ground pepper, stir and pour or brush evenly over the snoek.
5. Bake for about 30 minutes. Remove from the oven and baste with any leftover jam sauce.
6. Switch on the oven's grill and grill the snoek for 3–5 minutes to get a caramelised sheen. If the white, fleshy area flakes easily with a fork and the fish does not look raw, it is done. If you are unsure, leave it in the warm oven for another minute or three.
7. Serve with freshly baked bread spread with butter and apricot jam.

TIP This is also great done on the braai. I make a makeshift baking tray with heavy-duty aluminium foil and braai the snoek over medium-hot coals for about 45 minutes, basting continuously with the sweet juices that run off.

SOLE WITH BUTTERNUT MASH

I had only ever eaten sole in a restaurant. One day, when I was out shopping, right there on the ice at the fishmonger section of my favourite grocery store, were several flat fish peering at me with their squat eyes. They were soles and I knew I just had to try them. You can substitute any buttery, meaty fish, such as panga. Remember to get it filleted and skinned by the fishmonger.

80 MINUTES | SERVES **1**

INGREDIENTS
2 large soles, filleted
1 cup yoghurt or buttermilk
1 small butternut, peeled, halved and deseeded
2 small potatoes
salt and freshly ground black pepper to taste
butter for frying
1 cup fine breadcrumbs
1 tsp lemon juice
1 lemon wedge

WHAT TO DO
1. Marinate the soles in 200 ml yoghurt or buttermilk for about 30 minutes.
2. Meanwhile, make the mash. Boil the butternut and unpeeled potatoes in salted water for 30 minutes or until soft. Set aside to cool for 5 minutes.
3. Peel and slice the potatoes. Cut the potatoes and butternut into small pieces. Season with salt and add 1 tsp butter, along with some of the leftover yoghurt or buttermilk. Mash until smooth and set aside, keeping warm, until needed.
4. Tip the breadcrumbs onto a plate.
5. Melt a knob of butter in a hot frying pan. Take a sole by the tail, dip it into the breadcrumbs on both sides and immediately put it into the pan. If your pan can comfortably take both soles, cook them together.
6. Fry for about 2 minutes until the underside is golden, then turn the sole, add a little more butter and the lemon juice and fry for another 2 minutes, or until approaching a golden colour.
7. Serve the soles with a generous dollop of butternut mash, freshly ground black pepper and a lemon wedge.

> **TIP**   Butternut mash also works beautifully with pork chops or steak.

CATCH OF THE DAY

CALAMARI STEAKS WITH SWEET POTATO CHIPS

There is something unbelievably reassuring about having chips as part of a meal. I swear I could write a song for every time I get perfectly fried chips. Sweet potato chips go really well with calamari. Don't be scared (like I was); calamari is actually such an easy thing to cook. And well worth it! If you can't get fresh calamari steaks, defrosted from frozen is fine.

50 MINUTES | SERVES **1**

INGREDIENTS
2 medium cucumber-shaped sweet potatoes, well washed
2 calamari steaks
freshly ground black pepper to taste
juice of ½ lemon
olive oil
non-stick cooking spray
sprig of fresh thyme, chopped
1 tsp butter
1 clove garlic, peeled and very thinly sliced
salt to taste
1 lemon wedge

WHAT TO DO
1. Boil the unpeeled sweet potatoes in a pot of salted water for 7–10 minutes, depending on their size and thickness. Drain and leave to cool.
2. Wash the calamari steaks and pat dry. Score lightly and rub with freshly ground black pepper, the lemon juice and a glug of olive oil.
3. Preheat the oven to 200 °C. Grease a baking tray with non-stick cooking spray.
4. Cut the sweet potatoes into long thin chips. Drizzle with olive oil and sprinkle with most of the thyme. Mix gently to coat before spreading onto the baking tray. Bake for 30–40 minutes.
5. When the chips have about 10 minutes to go, heat a frying pan over high heat and add a little olive oil and the butter. Add the calamari steaks, the garlic and some salt. Fry the calamari for 2 minutes or until brown underneath, and then turn over and fry for another 2 minutes.
6. Grind some salt with the remaining thyme in a pestle and mortar and sprinkle over the chips before serving.
7. Serve the calamari steaks with the chips and a lemon wedge.

> TIP   Try the sweet potato chips with some kassler or lamb chops.

CATCH OF THE DAY

FRIED BABY SQUID WITH ZESTY ORANGE MASH

I love the contrast between the crisp baby squid and the silky orange mash. Food isn't just about taste and look, but also about texture. This dish assaults your mouth with two opposing textures but, strangely enough, it works! To serve as a starter for a dinner party just halve the portion and multiply it by how many people there are.

40 MINUTES | SERVES **1**

INGREDIENTS
1 medium potato
1 medium sweet potato
200 g baby squid
juice of ½ lemon
olive oil
½ tsp paprika
2 Tbsp cornflour
salt and freshly ground black pepper to taste
½ tsp butter
juice and zest of 1 orange
sunflower oil

WHAT TO DO
1. To make the mash, boil the potato and sweet potato in a pot of salted water for about 30 minutes until soft. Drain and leave until cool enough to handle.
2. Peel and dice the potatoes and mash with the butter, 1 tsp orange juice and a little orange zest. Season with salt to taste and set aside. Keep warm.
3. Mix the baby squid with the lemon juice, a glug of olive oil and the paprika. Sprinkle over the cornflour and season with salt and pepper. Mix thoroughly.
4. Heat about ½ cup equal parts sunflower oil and olive oil in a frying pan. When the oil is hot, add the squid quickly, one by one. Turn after a minute, every minute, for 3 minutes or until crispy.
5. Serve with a great big dollop of orange mash on the side.

> **TIP** This zesty orange mash makes a great accompaniment to braaied lamb.

CALAMARI RINGS WITH TARTARE SAUCE

This is a refreshing snack to munch on when you have mates over, or if you are having a movie marathon. The batter works well with thick-cut onion rings too. Enjoy!

20 MINUTES | SERVES **2**

INGREDIENTS
1 egg
1 cup beer (I use Windhoek Draught)
½ cup flour
½ cup cornflour
1 tsp salt
sprig of fresh rosemary, half the leaves finely chopped
½ cup mayonnaise
juice of ½ lemon
glug of olive oil
¾ cup finely shredded lettuce
2 spring onions, finely chopped
2–3 gherkins or peppadews, finely chopped
salt and freshly ground black pepper to taste
½ cup sunflower oil
2 calamari tubes, sliced into rings or 800 g calamari rings

WHAT TO DO
1. To make the batter, whisk the egg and gradually add the beer. Then add the flour, cornflour, salt and chopped rosemary.
2. To make the tartare sauce, mix the mayonnaise, lemon juice, olive oil, lettuce, spring onions and gherkins or peppadews. Season with salt and pepper to taste.
3. Heat the sunflower oil in a frying pan over high heat. When the oil is ready, dip the calamari rings into the batter and fry a few at a time, using a fork to turn them over as they brown. Drain on paper towel.
4. Grind the remaining rosemary with some salt in a pestle and mortar and use to season the calamari before serving with the tartare sauce.

CATCH OF THE DAY

SOMETHING MEATY

FOR THE INNER CARNIVORE

Although there is a growing trend towards veganism and vegetarianism, I am a staunch meat eater. I love the textures and tastes, and can't imagine a day without it! Here are a few recipes that should tickle more than a few taste buds. They'll also help you think about what else you can do with conventional cuts of meat.

PORK CHOPS WITH GINGER BEER

Pork and ginger go well together; try it for yourself and see how you like it!

60 MINUTES | SERVES **4**

INGREDIENTS
4 large pork chops
2 apples, peeled and sliced into thin half-moons
3 large carrots, peeled and julienned
2 star anise
salt and freshly ground black pepper to taste
2 cups (500ml) ginger beer

WHAT TO DO

1. Preheat the oven to 180 °C. Trim the pork chops of excess fat and rind, and grill them for 30 seconds each side. Then place in a casserole.
2. Cover and surround the chops with the apple slices and carrots. Add the star anise and season with salt and pepper. Pour over the ginger beer.
3. Cover with foil or a lid and cook for about 50 minutes.
4. Increase the heat to 220 °C. Remove the lid and cook the chops for a further 10 minutes to allow them to brown a bit.
5. Serve with a simple coleslaw (shred some red or green cabbage and carrots and combine with mayonnaise and a dash of freshly squeezed lemon juice).

> **TIP** If you want to make this dish sweeter, add a few tablespoons of spare-rib marinade or honey to the casserole before you put it into the oven.

SOMETHING MEATY

STICKY PORK RIBS

This Asian-inspired recipe works for any type of rib, be it pork, beef or lamb. The marinade really is finger-licking good, and easy to make!

1 HOUR | SERVES 1—2

INGREDIENTS
juice of 1 lemon
2 racks pork ribs (ask for short ribs, as they have more meat on them)
1 cup cider
⅓ cup soy sauce
⅓ cup honey
½ tsp finely chopped fresh garlic
pinch of cayenne pepper
1 star anise
½ cup brown or Demerara sugar
1 tsp freshly ground black pepper

WHAT TO DO
1. Squeeze the lemon juice over the pork ribs.
2. Add all the other ingredients to a large pot and stir until mostly dissolved.
3. Cut the ribs to fit the pot, then add them, cover the pot with a lid and simmer over medium heat for 40 minutes.
4. Remove the ribs from the pot and reduce the marinade to a runny syrup.
5. Preheat the oven to 200 °C.
6. Transfer the ribs to a baking dish or casserole, and add the marinade a tablespoon at a time, every 5 minutes, for 20 minutes.
7. Switch on the grill for the last 5 minutes to get a good caramelisation going.
8. Cut the ribs into individual riblets and serve with the reduced marinade poured over.

> TIP   If you have the time, cook the ribs in the pot for longer — the meat will get even softer and sweeter, and the sauce thicker.
> Don't use smoked ribs, or the dish will be too salty.

SOMETHING MEATY

T-BONE STEAK WITH STRAWBERRY JAM

There are many things I can be accused of, and marrying strange flavours is one of them. This is one of my favourite quick recipes for a lazy autumn evening. Try it out.

15 MINUTES | SERVES 2

INGREDIENTS
olive oil
2 thick-cut T-bone steaks
dollop of butter
salt and freshly ground black pepper to taste
½ cup organic strawberry jam
1 tsp whole Madagascar green peppercorns

WHAT TO DO
1. Heat some olive oil in a large frying pan. When it starts to smoke, add a dollop of butter and the T-bone steaks. Season with salt and pepper and fry for 3 minutes before turning. Fry for another 3 minutes and turn again.
2. Add the strawberry jam and green peppercorns to the pan and cook for a further 2 minutes until the jam caramelises onto the steaks.
3. Rest the steaks for 5 minutes before serving.

> **TIP** Serve the steak with chips (see page 67) or butternut mash (see page 97). You can use most steak cuts. T-bones cook a bit faster since the bone relays the heat to the meat.

TERIYAKI STEAK

Asian flavours and red meat go amazingly well together. In this recipe, a few simple ingredients deliver something surprisingly delicious.

15 MINUTES | SERVES **2**

INGREDIENTS
sunflower oil
2 aged sirloin steaks
salt and freshly ground black pepper to taste
150 ml teriyaki sauce
2 carrots, peeled and julienned
handful of baby spinach, blanched or steamed

WHAT TO DO

1. Heat some sunflower oil in a frying pan over high heat. Add the steaks, season with salt and pepper and fry for 3 minutes on each side (they should be rare to medium rare).
2. Remove from the heat and add 100 ml teriyaki sauce to the pan, swirling it around to coat the steaks. Leave to rest for at least 5 minutes.
3. Microwave the carrots for 3 minutes on high until soft but still crunchy.
4. Slice the steaks, reserving the pan juices.
5. Arrange the baby spinach on two plates. Top with the carrots and slices of steak and drizzle over the meat juices and remaining teriyaki sauce.

TIP This dish is delicious served with some egg or rice noodles.

SOMETHING MEATY

TRINCHADO

This has to be one the best ways of cooking meat I have ever come across. You are basically poaching the meat in a broth, locking in its flavours while keeping it soft and juicy. You can use minute steak or any cheaper cut of beef instead of the sirloin. Serve with some corn on the cob for an authentic student experience!

80 MINUTES | SERVES 2

INGREDIENTS
4 cups boiling water
4 tsp beef stock powder or 2 cubes
1 onion, peeled and finely diced
1 heaped tsp chopped fresh garlic
4 bay leaves
glug of Worcestershire or soy sauce
1 cup white wine
pinch of cayenne pepper or dried chilli flakes
2 Tbsp tomato paste
freshly ground black pepper to taste
2 sirloin steaks
olive oil

WHAT TO DO
1. Boil the water in a large pot over high heat, add the stock powder and stir until it dissolves. Add the onion, garlic and bay leaves. Lower the heat to medium and simmer for 10 minutes.
2. Add the Worcestershire or soy sauce, white wine, cayenne pepper or chilli flakes and tomato paste. Stir, and simmer for another 10 minutes. Add black pepper to taste and simmer for a further 30 minutes.
3. Heat a frying pan over very high heat. Smear the steaks with olive oil and sear for 60–90 seconds on each side to get a good colour. Remove from the pan – the steaks should still be very rare – and leave to rest on a plate.
4. When the sauce is ready, probably after another 10 minutes of simmering, slice the steaks into bite-sized strips. Add the meat juices to the pot, then add the steak strips.
5. Poach the steak in the sauce for 1–2 minutes. Don't overcook it.
6. Serve with mealies and buttered fresh Portuguese rolls.

> **TIP** If using minute steaks, cut them into thin strips and add to the broth without frying first – the poaching will be enough to cook them.

SOMETHING MEATY

MUTTON BREDIE

There is nothing that says comfort like a bredie. Make it for yourself, for your mates or for a random Sunday kuier *when your flatmate brings home some mutton from the family farm. I have often made a discount on mutton an excuse to make a bredie – so should you!*

2 HOURS | SERVES **4–6**

INGREDIENTS
1 kg mutton, roughly chopped
salt and freshly ground black pepper to taste
1 Tbsp butter
4 onions, peeled and quartered
4 carrots, peeled and sliced into 2 cm-thick chunks
4 potatoes, peeled and quartered
handful of green beans, topped, tailed and halved
2 tsp mutton stock powder
2 tsp curry powder
3 bay leaves
1 Tbsp sugar
2 cups boiling water, or 1 cup water and 1 cup chardonnay
sprig of fresh rosemary

WHAT TO DO
1. Preheat the oven to 180 °C.
2. Season the mutton with salt and pepper.
3. Melt the butter in a large frying pan over high heat and brown the meat.
4. Place the browned meat in a casserole along with the onions, carrots, potatoes and green beans.
5. Add the stock powder, curry powder, bay leaves and sugar to the boiling water and pour over the mutton and vegetables. Break the rosemary over the contents, season with salt and pepper and cover with the lid.
6. Cook for 1 hour and 30 minutes.
7. Remove the lid and cook for a further 20 minutes. If you want to thicken the sauce, dissolve 1 tsp cornflour in ½ cup milk and add to the casserole 15–20 minutes before cooking is complete.
8. Serve with steamed basmati rice.

> **TIP** Bredies are usually better the day after you make them – they are more sweet and tasty. And they're also great to eat cold. Try it!

SOMETHING MEATY

SWEET THINGS

TO (BAKE) FOR

No day is complete without something sweet. This is especially true for a student, where a rusk or slice of tart can be relegated to sainthood when presented at the right time. With my help you won't have to wait for the kindness of a *tannie* or your parents before you get to taste something sweet and homemade again.

PAVLOVA

You might ask yourself what a pavlova recipe is doing in a beginners' cookbook, or even 'What is a pavlova?' It really is a simple dessert to make, and it always impresses!

2 HOURS | SERVES 8

INGREDIENTS
8 eggs, separated
500 g castor sugar
4 tsp cornflour
½ tsp vanilla extract
2 tsp white vinegar
whipped cream or fresh custard, seasonal fresh berries, figs,
    honey and nuts to serve

WHAT TO DO
1. Preheat the oven to 180 °C. Line a baking tray with baking paper.
2. Whisk the egg whites in a large bowl until soft peaks form. (Store the yolks in a plastic container in the fridge or use them to make chocolate custard for the pavlova.)
3. Add the castor sugar, a tablespoon at a time, and continue whisking until all the sugar is incorporated and stiff peaks form.
4. Sift over the cornflour, add the vanilla extract and vinegar and fold into the mixture.
5. Use a metal spoon to make a large circular meringue on the lined baking tray.
6. Lower the oven's temperature to 120 °C and bake the meringue for 50 minutes. Then switch off the oven but leave the meringue to cool in the warm oven for 1 hour.
7. Plate the meringue, fill with whipped cream or custard, and top with fresh berries, quartered figs, honey and nuts.

> TIP   To make individual pavlovas, make smaller meringue circles and cook them for 30 minutes instead of 50 minutes.

CREMORA TART

I will not easily forget the first time I had Cremora tart. I was staying in res, visiting a friend's home for the weekend, and his mum made it for us. It was one of the most profound taste sensations – sour and sweet, but not as in-your-face as lemon meringue.

2 HOURS | SERVES 12

INGREDIENTS
50 g salted butter
1 x 200 g pkt tennis biscuits, finely crushed
1 x 250 g pkt Cremora
1 cup hot water
2 x 385 g cans condensed milk
1 cup lemon juice
toasted pumpkin seeds (optional) and honey to serve

WHAT TO DO
1. Melt the butter in a cup in the microwave and mix with the tennis biscuits. Use this to line the bottom of a tart tin or pie dish. Place in the fridge to set.
2. Whisk the Cremora into the hot water until completely dissolved. Cool to room temperature.
3. Whisk the condensed milk and the Cremora water in a mixing bowl. Start adding the lemon juice, a little at a time, whisking until the mixture thickens considerably – you will most likely not use all the lemon juice.
4. Pour the filling onto the tart base, level with a spatula and place in the fridge to cool and set.
5. Scatter over some toasted pumpkin seeds, if desired, and drizzle with honey before serving.

> **TIP** For a creamier and less sweet tart, substitute a tub of smooth cottage cheese for one of the condensed milk cans.

SWEET THINGS

GINGER & OAT SNAPS

Cookies are non-negotiable.

50 MINUTES | MAKES ABOUT **40**

INGREDIENTS
2 cups cake flour
1 cup brown or Demerara sugar
½ tsp salt
2 tsp ground ginger
½ tsp baking soda
1 tsp ground cinnamon
1 cup rolled oats
140 g unsalted butter
2 eggs
1 tsp honey or syrup

WHAT TO DO

1. Preheat the oven to 180 °C. Line a baking tray with baking paper.
2. Sift all the dry ingredients into a large mixing bowl. Add the oats and then mix in the butter with your fingertips.
3. Whisk the eggs with the honey or syrup, and add to the flour mixture. Mix well to form a dough – don't worry if it seems dry, it mustn't be wet.
4. Break off bits of dough and form into balls, roughly golf ball size. Place the balls in rows on the baking tray and gently flatten them. Leave space between the balls to allow the biscuits to expand as they cook.
5. Bake for 15–20 minutes until golden in colour. Allow to cool before storing in an airtight container.

> **TIP** To make peanut butter cookies, add two tablespoons of peanut butter to the batter instead of the ground ginger.

SWEET THINGS

CHOCOLATE GANACHE TRUFFLES

Before stumbling upon this recipe from a very old French cookery book, I always thought making truffles was bloody hard! Then I saw that you basically need only three ingredients and you get to play with your food – and I was sold! Now I make truffles for special occasions and even freeze them. You simply thaw them in the fridge. Yes – you too can make your own truffles!

1 HOUR | MAKES ABOUT 30

INGREDIENTS
90 ml thick cream
1 heaped Tbsp salted butter
200 g dark chocolate, finely chopped
½ cup roasted hazelnuts
¼ cup cocoa powder

WHAT TO DO
1. Heat the cream and butter in a saucepan over high heat, stirring continuously. Take it off the heat as soon as it is about to boil. Add to a mixing bowl with the chocolate and stir until the chocolate has melted and all is thoroughly combined.
2. Allow the ganache mixture to cool to room temperature. It should now be thick enough to roll into balls.
3. Sift the cocoa powder onto a plate. Using a hazelnut as the centre, take a heaped tablespoon of ganache and quickly roll it around the hazelnut to form a ball. Be careful not to let your body heat melt the ganache.
4. Roll in the cocoa powder to cover it and place on a sheet of wax paper.
5. Continue until you have used up all the ganache. Store the truffles in an airtight container in the fridge or freezer, separating the layers with wax paper.

> **TIP** These truffles are soft because they are made from a ganache. If you want, you can use a toothpick and dip them into some melted dark chocolate to give them a hard chocolate shell. Or try rolling them in desiccated coconut or even chopped nuts. Add extra butter and cream to the recipe for a smoother, mousse-like ganache that you can use as a topping for cakes and cupcakes.

SWEET THINGS

DECADENT CHOCOLATE FONDANTS

Chocolate fondants are a guilty pleasure. Breaking into that warm, soft cocoa sponge with your fork or spoon to reveal the most amazing, chocolatey ooze is what defines this dessert. This is a quick and easy recipe that I just love.

1 HOUR | MAKES 4

INGREDIENTS
2 Tbsp butter, at room temperature
2 Tbsp cocoa powder
100 g 70% dark chocolate, chopped
100 g salted butter, diced
100 g Demerara or brown sugar
2 eggs
2 egg yolks
100 g cake flour

WHAT TO DO
1. Use small ramekins if you have them (if you only have large ones, add 3–5 minutes to the cooking time). Alternatively, use a muffin pan lined with cupcake papers. Grease 4 ramekins with the 2 Tbsp butter (also the cupcake papers if you are using them). Dust the insides with the cocoa powder to cover the butter. Place in the fridge or freezer while you make the batter.
2. Microwave the chocolate in a microwaveable bowl on high for 10 second intervals until the majority of the chocolate has melted. Add the butter and use a metal spoon to combine. Microwave for a further 10 seconds if necessary. Stir until smooth and then set aside.
3. In a separate bowl, combine the sugar, eggs and egg yolks. Whisk for about 2 minutes until the sugar has mostly dissolved, then sift over the flour and lightly fold it into the mixture with a metal spoon.
4. Now slowly fold in the chocolate mixture until well mixed.
5. Chill the batter in the fridge for 30 minutes or even overnight, depending on when you want to serve the fondants. Preheat the oven to 200 °C when you are ready to bake.
6. Divide the batter evenly between the ramekins and bake for 10–12 minutes. The fondants are done when the tops are spongy and the sides have started pulling away from the ramekins.
7. Rest for a few minutes before serving, as they will shrink a little and be easier to remove.
8. Carefully loosen the sides with a flat knife and place on warmed serving plates. Serve with either a very dark, very cocoa-ey chocolate sauce, or a light vanilla ice cream or cream.

> **TIP**   You can easily double this recipe to make more (you'll want to).

SWEET THINGS

EASY PANCAKES

This recipe is so simple and easy to remember – you will be able to save the day without needing a cookbook by your side!

20 MINUTES **|** MAKES **10–12**

INGREDIENTS
1 cup cake flour
1 heaped tsp baking powder
1 tsp sugar
pinch of salt
2 small eggs
2 cups milk
sunflower oil
cinnamon sugar to serve

WHAT TO DO
1. Sift the flour, baking powder, sugar and salt into a mixing bowl. Whisk the eggs with 1 cup milk and add to the dry ingredients. The batter should be quite runny, like pouring cream, so add more milk if you need to.
2. Let the batter rest in the fridge while you heat ½ tsp oil in a non-stick frying pan on high.
3. Ladle some batter into the pan and quickly swirl it around to cover the surface. After about 30 seconds bubbles will start to appear on the pancake's surface and the batter will no longer be runny. Flip the pancake and cook for 30 seconds on the other side.
4. Slide the cooked pancake onto a plate and sprinkle with cinnamon sugar. Repeat with the rest of the batter, stacking the pancakes and adding some cinnamon sugar to each layer. The sugar will dissolve into a thin, cinnamon-rich syrup. Roll the pancakes when you are ready to eat.

> **TIP**   Add a dash of lemon juice for a rather surprising taste explosion!

SWEET THINGS

PIECE-OF-CAKE CHOCOLATE CAKE

This is a no-fuss, one-bowl, moist and delicious chocolate cake. The list of ingredients might seem long, but when you taste the cake, you'll know it was worth the effort.

1 HOUR | SERVES 12

INGREDIENTS
2 eggs
1 cup buttermilk or milk
1 tsp vanilla extract
2 cups Demerara or brown sugar
½ cup melted unsalted butter or sunflower oil
2 cups cake flour
¾ cup cocoa powder
½ Tbsp baking powder
2 tsp bicarbonate of soda
pinch of salt
1 cup warm coffee

ICING
50 g smooth cream cheese
150 g unsalted butter, softened
½ cup icing sugar
½ cup cocoa powder
½ cup strawberry jam

WHAT TO DO
1. Preheat the oven to 180 °C. Grease two 23 cm-diameter cake pans or three 20 cm-diameter cake pans.
2. Combine the eggs, buttermilk or milk, vanilla extract, sugar and butter or oil in a large mixing bowl. Whisk for 2 minutes until well mixed.
3. Sift over the flour, cocoa powder, baking powder, bicarbonate of soda and salt, and mix well.
4. Lastly, add the warm coffee and mix well.
5. Divide the batter between the cake pans and bake for 35 minutes. Check to see whether they are done by inserting a skewer into their centres. It should come out clean.
6. Allow the cakes to rest for 10 minutes before loosening the sides with a flat knife. After another 10 minutes turn out the cakes onto a wire rack.
7. To make the icing, combine the cream cheese and butter in a mixing bowl. Sift over the icing sugar and cocoa powder and mix well. Refrigerate until the cakes are cool enough to ice.
8. Sandwich the cakes together with strawberry jam and ice the top.

TIP To make cupcakes: bake for 20–25 minutes in a cupcake or muffin pan. When cool, slice them in half, sandwich with strawberry jam and ice the tops.

SWEET THINGS

MICROWAVE CAKE-IN-A-MUG

Sometimes we just want to be able to press a button and make a cake magically appear. Using a microwave to bake a cake is probably the closest you'll come to instant gratification, bar buying a cake from your local bakery. Just whip the ingredients together and press power! I will not lie and say it's superior to an oven-baked cake, but it sure is handy if you want chocolate cake and you want it NOW! Make this with friends in mind, although the batter will keep for up to three days in the fridge.

10 MINUTES | SERVES **2**

INGREDIENTS
1 egg
1 egg yolk
3 Tbsp buttermilk or full-cream milk
3 Tbsp melted salted butter or sunflower oil
¼ cup brown or Demerara sugar
¼ cup cake flour
2 heaped Tbsp sifted cocoa powder
3 Tbsp dark chocolate chips or chopped dark chocolate

WHAT TO DO
1. Mix all the wet ingredients in a mixing bowl.
2. Add the sugar, followed by the flour and cocoa powder. Mix well.
3. Lastly, add the chocolate.
4. Pour into oversized mugs, filling them to about three-quarters full.
5. Microwave each on high for 5 minutes, letting them rest in the microwave for at least 5 minutes before removing them.

> **TIP** Serve this as a warm pudding: remove from the mug and drench in cream or custard. Double the recipe to serve 4.

SWEET THINGS

BANANA BREAD

I have a confession to make. I have an itchy trigger finger when it comes to buying fruit. I often find that my half grocery bag is filled with fresh apples, guavas and bananas, and I don't always have the time or inclination to eat them all. I made up this recipe out of necessity, as my kitchen was starting to smell like a banana-farm! And now I buy extra bananas on purpose just so that I have a reason to make this great banana bread! You can also use the batter to make muffins if you haven't got loaf tins. Just reduce the baking time to 25–30 minutes.

1 HOUR | MAKES 2 LOAVES

INGREDIENTS
½ cup brown or Demerara sugar
100 g salted butter, softened
1 egg
½ cup full-fat Bulgarian yoghurt or buttermilk
1½ cups cake flour
2 tsp baking powder
½ tsp bicarbonate of soda
4 overripe bananas, peeled and mashed
2 cups crushed All-Bran flakes or muesli/granola, or a mixture
1 tsp vanilla essence

WHAT TO DO
1. Cream the sugar, butter, egg and yoghurt or buttermilk in a large mixing bowl. Sift over the flour, baking powder and bicarbonate of soda and mix.
2. Now add the remaining ingredients and mix well. Leave to rest in the fridge for at least 10 minutes.
3. When ready to bake, preheat the oven to 180 °C. Grease 2 medium loaf tins.
4. Divide the batter between the loaf tins and bake for 30–35 minutes.
5. Leave to cool in the tins before turning out onto a wire rack to cool completely. Store in the fridge or freezer in tinfoil. Serve with butter.

> **TIP** Use leftover banana bread to make a pudding: smear slices with jam and layer in a small casserole or baking dish. Pour over a mixture of 3 eggs, 1 cup milk and ½ cup sugar, and bake for 35–40 minutes at 180 °C until set. Serve with custard.

SWEET THINGS

CARROT & BANANA MUFFINS

These moist, healthy muffins make a lovely quick breakfast snack when you're on the run.

1 HOUR | MAKES 12–15

INGREDIENTS
2 cups cake flour
2 tsp baking powder
½ tsp ground allspice
½ tsp ground cinnamon
½ tsp ground nutmeg
1 cup brown or Demarara sugar
⅓ cup pumpkin seeds, finely chopped
½ cup melted butter
3 Tbsp sunflower oil
4 eggs
2 large carrots, peeled and grated
4 overripe bananas, peeled and mashed

WHAT TO DO
1. Preheat the oven to 180 °C. Grease a muffin pan.
2. Sift all the dry ingredients into a large mixing bowl. Add the seeds.
3. Add the butter, oil and 3 of the eggs to the dry ingredients. Add the carrot and banana and mix well. If the batter is too wet, add a little extra flour; if too dry, add the extra egg and a little more butter.
4. Spoon the batter into the holes of the muffin pan, half-filling them. Bake for 20–25 minutes. The muffins are done when a toothpick inserted into the centre of a muffin comes out clean.

> TIP   Try this recipe with any other fruit that you have too much of — just boil in sugar water until soft, mash and add instead of the banana.

SWEET THINGS

CHEESY JAM TARTS

This was one of my first creations. It made me realise that I might be onto something really tasty in my experiments with some well-known recipes. Try this the moment the weather starts going grey; its almost as soothing as pancakes, and they keep longer in the fridge!

35 MINUTES | MAKES 24

INGREDIENTS
500 g cake flour, plus extra if needed
5 tsp baking powder
½ tsp salt
125 g unsalted butter, at room temperature
1 cup finely grated mild Cheddar cheese
300 ml fresh full-cream milk
½ cup apricot jam
1 egg yolk whisked with 2 tsp milk

WHAT TO DO
1. Sift all the dry ingredients into a large mixing bowl.
2. Add the butter and use your fingertips to mix it into the flour.
3. Add the cheese and milk. Mix thoroughly, first with a wooden spoon and then with your hands, to form a dough. Add extra flour if the dough is too sticky – about 1 Tbsp should be enough.
4. Roll the dough into a sausage shape and divide into three. Cover 2 portions with clingfilm while you roll out the third to the shape of a large pizza, but not too thin.
5. Preheat the oven to 200 °C. Grease 2 baking trays with butter.
6. Slice the rolled-out dough into 8 'pizza' slices. Place 1 tsp jam in the centre of the wide end of each slice, then wet the sides of the triangle to the tip with just enough water to help make them stick (use a brush). Roll the slice from the wide end to the tip, using a little more pressure around the area of the jam in the centre to keep the jam contained. Place the rolled tart on a baking tray.
7. Repeat with the remaining slices before rolling out the other 2 portions of dough. Space the tarts at least 2 cm apart on the baking trays.
8. Lightly brush the tarts with the egg mixture before baking for 15 minutes or until golden brown.

TIP These keep very well in an airtight container in the fridge. I've even frozen them. Defrost slowly and then warm in the oven for 10 minutes before guests arrive. Try berry jams with Edam or white Gouda cheese. You can also use this recipe to make traditional crescent-shaped jam tartlets.

SWEET THINGS

SWEET PUMPKIN CROISSANTS

Yes, I know it sounds weird. But trust me, it works! The pumpkin flesh gives the croissants a gorgeous, natural orange-yellow colour, and helps keep them both moist and flavourful. Baking with yeast also makes this a proper, tasty treat – although it takes some time for the yeast to rise and create the air pockets that make these so light. Make a large batch and freeze them after you've baked them. When in the mood for a pumpkin delight, simply thaw and warm in the oven for 10 minutes.

TAKES TIME | MAKES **24**

INGREDIENTS
250 g cooked pumpkin or butternut
1 heaped Tbsp butter
1 kg all-purpose flour
10 g instant dried yeast
70 g brown, caramel, treacle or Demerara sugar (the darker, the more flavourful)
1 tsp salt
150 g butter
2 eggs, whisked
400 ml lukewarm water

WHAT TO DO
1. Mash the pumpkin with the 1 heaped Tbsp butter, and set aside to cool.
2. Sift all the dry ingredients into a large mixing bowl and use your fingertips to mix in the butter.
3. Add the eggs and water to the pumpkin, and add this to the flour mixture. Mix to form a dough.
4. Knead the dough for a few minutes with your hands and then leave in the mixing bowl, covered, in a warm place, to double in size.
5. Knead again and divide into 3 equal portions.
6. Roll out each portion to about the size of a large pizza (not too thin though).
7. Cut each dough 'pizza' into 8 slices. Roll each slice into a croissant by rolling from the wide end to the pointed end. Stick down the point with a drop of water and slightly bend the edges of the croissant inwards towards the point, creating that characteristic crescent shape.
8. Place the croissants on baking trays, leaving 2 cm between each, and leave in a warm place to double in size.
9. When almost ready to bake, preheat the oven to 200 °C.
10. Bake the croissants for about 20 minutes or until golden brown.

> TIP   You can also use this dough to make tasty scones. Serve warm with cream cheese and jam.

CHOCOLATE MOUSSE

Chocolate mousse used to be popular in restaurants, but I don't see it on menus any more. So sad really, because it is one of the best, easiest desserts to make!

30 MINUTES | SERVES **4—8**

INGREDIENTS
170 g dark chocolate
4 egg whites
¼ tsp lemon juice or white wine vinegar
40 g castor sugar

WHAT TO DO
1. You can microwave the chocolate in a glass mixing bowl for 10 seconds at a time and mix until it is all melted, or you can melt it the proper way over a pot of simmering water, letting the heat from the steam melt the chocolate slowly.
2. Whisk the egg whites until soft peaks form, then add the lemon juice or white wine vinegar and half the castor sugar, adding the rest as you whisk until stiff peaks form.
3. Add ⅓ of the egg white mixture quickly to the melted chocolate and mix thoroughly. Now fold this into the rest of the egg white mixture until thoroughly incorporated.
4. Spoon the mousse into your serving bowls or glasses and refrigerate for 3 hours until set.

> **TIP** Add some chilli flakes or flaked salt to the mixture to help bring out the chocolate flavour.

SWEET THINGS

RUSKS

These failsafe rusks always caused a stir in my student apartment. I couldn't keep up with the steady stream of guests in winter when word got round that I'd done some baking. I suggest keeping the recipe to yourself ...

TAKES TIME | MAKES ABOUT **100**

INGREDIENTS
1 kg self-raising flour
½ tsp salt
2 cups brown sugar
3 cups crushed All-Bran flakes
½ cup sunflower seeds, crushed
½ cup pumpkin seeds, crushed
2 tsp aniseed
1 cup toasted rolled oats or muesli or another cup All-Bran
500 g unsalted butter
1 egg
2 cups buttermilk, or 1 cup buttermilk and 1 cup Bulgarian yoghurt

WHAT TO DO
1. Preheat the oven to 180 °C. Grease 2 baking trays.
2. Sift the flour, salt and sugar into a large mixing bowl. Add the All-Bran, seeds and oats or muesli. Using your fingers, rub the butter into the mixture until thoroughly combined.
3. Whisk the egg in a mixing bowl and add the cultured milk. Pour this into the flour mixture and mix thoroughly with a wooden spoon.
4. Divide the dough into 2 equal parts and spread each onto a baking tray. Cut rusk shapes with a sharp serrated knife. Bake for 30–40 minutes until risen and golden, and the sides pull away from the baking trays.
5. Cut along the rusks again and allow to cool for 10 minutes before turning out of the trays and separating.
6. Reheat the oven to 100 °C. Place the rusks on an oven rack and leave in the oven with the door ajar for 90 minutes to dry out.
7. Allow the rusks to reach room temperature before storing them in an airtight container.

> TIP   I often add some of my muesli (see page 25) to this recipe, as well as raisins when baking for people who like them. I always keep some Nutty-Wheat flour handy to add to the dough if it is too wet.

INDEX

CONVERSION TABLE	
METRIC	IMPERIAL
Teaspoons	
2 ml	$1/4$ tsp
3 ml	$1/2$ tsp
5 ml	1 tsp
10 ml	2 tsp
20 ml	4 tsp
Tablespoons	
15 ml	1 Tbsp
30 ml	2 Tbsp
45 ml	3 Tbsp
Cups	
60 ml	$1/4$ cup
80 ml	$1/3$ cup
125 ml	$1/2$ cup
160 ml	$2/3$ cup
200 ml	$3/4$ cup
250 ml	1 cup
375 ml	$1 1/2$ cups
500 ml	2 cups
1 litre	4 cups